THE
COOKWARE COOKBOOK

THE
COOKWARE COOKBOOK

BY **JAMÉE RUTH**
PHOTOGRAPHS BY LEIGH BEISCH

great recipes for broiling, steaming,
boiling, poaching, braising, deglazing, frying,
simmering, and sautéing

CHRONICLE BOOKS
SAN FRANCISCO

Library of Congress Cataloging-in-Publication Data available.

ISBN 0-8118-4236-3

Manufactured in China.

Photo assistance by Angelica Cao

Prop styling by Sara Slavin

Food styling by Dan Becker

Food styling assistance by Lou Bustamante

Designed by LushDesign / Eliza Bullock

Illustrations by LushDesign / Eliza Bullock

Typesetting by LushDesign / Eliza Bullock

The photographer wishes to thank Heath Ceramics for their
generous lending of tableware and pots.

Distributed in Canada by Raincoast Books

9050 Shaughnessy Street

Vancouver, British Columbia V6P 6E5

10 9 8 7 6 5 4 3 2 1

Chronicle Books LLC

85 Second Street

San Francisco, California 94105

www.chroniclebooks.com

acknowledgments

I consider myself very fortunate and am grateful to those people who enrich my life with generosity, talent, and love. ☐ Lots of love to my mummy, Janeé; my father, George; Aimée; Steve; and a special thank you to Marc and Wendy for saving my life. Mimi, I wish you were here to share this with me. ☐ To my dear friend Andrew Getty, a long overdue thank you for encouraging me to write many years ago and for sharing your unique wit and remarkable vocabulary. ☐ Editor Deborah Kops, what a pleasure to work and learn from you again! ☐ I am privileged to be a Chronicle Books author surrounded by the finest guidance and talent. My editor, Bill LeBlond, I thank you for your continued support and extraordinary enthusiasm. Amy Treadwell, you constantly amaze me with your knowledge and creativity. You are invaluable and I hope to work with you on many more books. ☐ My sincere appreciation to the team at Chronicle Books: art director Julia Flagg, for another uniquely designed book that I can be proud of; Eliza Bullock, for design, typesetting, and illustration; Jan Hughes and Doug Ogan for additional editing and their remarkable attention to detail; and Alan Watt, who directed production. ☐ I am very impressed by photographer Leigh Beisch, who managed to capture such stunningly beautiful pictures of my recipes along with her team: assistant Angelica Cao, food stylist Dan Becker, and the very talented prop stylist Sara Slavin. ☐ For continuing to supply me with premium culinary equipment I am grateful to All-Clad Metalcrafters; Wüsthof-Trident of America; KitchenAid; Le Creuset of America; Lodge Manufacturing Company; and Rösle.

contents

Ever since the first clay pots were made fourteen thousand years ago in today's Japan, we have been perfecting our cookware. These days the home cook can choose from an astonishing variety of pots and pans. A simple fry pan—the workhorse of the kitchen—

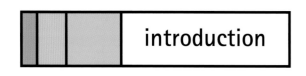

introduction

comes in several sizes and assorted metals, from old-fashioned cast iron to the more sleek clad stainless steel. In addition to everyday pans, cookware stores are filled with items that are designed for special uses, such as French fish poachers, asparagus pots, and shallow, loop-handled paella pans, made for the famous Spanish dish of the same name.

Making your way through this culinary bazaar can be overwhelming. I will help you select the pots and pans you need—in the store, when you are shopping, and even more importantly, in the kitchen, when you may be wondering which pan is best for turning out crispy, yet succulent 'Tucky Fried Chicken, deliciously decadent Chocolate Mousse, or dozens of other tasty dishes. Finally, I'll show you how to take care of your cookware so that you will have it for years to come.

The recipes in this cookbook were chosen to showcase a wide variety of pots and pans, demonstrate the kitchen tasks for which each one is best suited, and the importance of using the right one. These tempting dishes will also help you expand your culinary repertoire, and encourage you to increase your arsenal of equipment. Thanks to your cast-iron fry pan, Lumptious Crab Cakes will be crispy on the outside and tender on the inside. Your stockpot will become a seductive bucket of clams with a tasty broth begging to be soaked up by a crusty loaf of bread when you make Surf's Up Steamers. Your family and guests will clean their plates when you serve a batch of Keep It Coming Tempura from your trusty wok. If you don't own one already, you may be inspired to buy a marmite, an enameled cast-iron cauldron (sometimes called a "bouillabaisse pot"), so that your Fresh Catch Bouillabaisse or By You Gumbo cooks slowly and evenly to produce a bewitching stew. And for those silky ribbons of Lover's Linguine and Shells, nothing works better than a pasta pentola, a large, handsome pot with a strainer insert. No more carrying a heavy pot of boiling water to the colander in the sink and getting a face full of steam as you drain the pasta!

Whether you're steaming, boiling, poaching, braising, deglazing, frying, simmering, or sautéing, *The Cookware Cookbook* will guide and inspire you, the home cook, to achieve culinary success.

If cared for properly, a cast-iron skillet used during the Civil War would be as useful today as it was in 1861. The same is true of a hand-hammered, high-carbon steel wok. Quality lasts. □ Most manufacturers specialize by making a line of pots and pans from

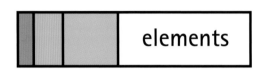

elements

the same material. Thanks to modern technology, some of these pots and pans are actually made from a composition of materials. One of the most successful is clad stainless steel—a copper or aluminum core sandwiched between layers of stainless steel. □ As you will see from the descriptions that follow, each substance used to make pots and pans has something to offer the home cook. Heat conductivity is the most important quality to keep in mind when selecting a pot or pan. Cast iron conducts and retains heat beautifully, which is why I wouldn't make fried chicken in anything else. A cast-iron pan coated with enamel doesn't conduct heat quite as well, but it's ideal for slow cooking. When you cook with acidic foods such as tomatoes and wine, make sure the interiors of your pots and pans are nonreactive, which means they will not give your food a metallic taste or alter the color.

aluminum

Not many companies produce pure aluminum cookware anymore. It is a fantastic heat conductor, but reacts to acidic foods. To clean aluminum cookware, wash with hot soapy water and scour if necessary, then rinse well and dry immediately.

anodized aluminum

Several manufacturers have perfected the electro-chemical process that has made aluminum very durable and nearly nonreactive to acidic foods. It is either plain with a matte or polished surface or dark gray like calphalon. Anodized aluminum pots will not chip or stain and scratch only when mistreated with a metal utensil, but they will get spotty and fade over time, especially if you do the unthinkable and clean them in the dishwasher. Instead, clean them with a nylon scrub pad—never steel wool—and hot soapy water. Rinse very well and dry immediately. If the interior starts to get spotty or fades, it is not damaged. Simply fill the pan with water and a little white vinegar and boil for about fifteen minutes. Then wash with soapy water, rinse well, and dry immediately.

cast iron

Some people cook with cast-iron pots and pans that are over one hundred years old. They seem to last forever. This metal absorbs, conducts, and retains heat like nothing else, which makes it ideal for frying and blackening. You can easily recognize the heavy black ironware; it is widely available and not too pricey. The interior must be seasoned, which is simple once you get the hang of it. Generously coat the inside with vegetable oil, put the pan in the oven, and set it at 350°F. Leave the pan in the oven for an hour. Then remove and allow to cool to room temperature. When storing cast iron, I like to line the inside with plastic wrap to keep it clean. Depending on how often you use it, cast iron needs to be reseasoned only occasionally. To clean, use light soap and hot water, or scrub with coarse salt and a soft sponge. Do not use strong cleansers. Rinse your pan well and wipe dry with a paper towel, then lightly coat the interior with a little oil. Never let this durable cookware sit with water inside, or it will rust. If you discover rust spots, use a nylon scrub sponge with a little soap and water to clean, then dry well and reseason.

clad stainless steel

My favorite! Most chefs prefer this combination of materials because it is suitable for cooking just about any dish. A clad metal pot is made of either aluminum or copper—both great heat conductors—sandwiched between two sheets of stainless steel. The result is a handsome, durable pot that heats quickly and evenly and is easy to care for. The best way to preserve and use your clad stainless steel pan is to wipe it with oil before you begin to cook. This ensures that the metal will stay moist and nothing will stick. You can use virtually any type of utensil when cooking in a pot with a clad stainless steel interior. Do not be afraid to get rough. Let the pan get beat up a bit. To restore its good looks, the best cleaning product I have found is called Bar Keepers Friend, available at most supermarkets in the cleaning products section. A paste made of this powder and a little water will refresh your pan and make it look like new. Make sure to then wash the pan with hot soapy water, rinse very well, and dry immediately.

copper

This is the most expensive cookware and the hardest to take care of, but oh so pretty! I do not recommend having lots of copper pots and pans, but cream- and egg-based sauces emerge from a copper pot so much creamier, the difference is remarkable. I also recommend a copper mixing bowl. Because of a chemical reaction between egg whites and copper, eggs whisked in one of these bowls come out so fluffy that your omelet will be like a cloud. Copper pots and pans are lined with either tin or, better, stainless steel to keep them from reacting to acidic foods and to prevent the copper, which is toxic, from leaching into the food (using an unlined copper bowl occasionally will not harm you however). Wash your copper pans with hot soapy water and dry immediately. The exterior needs to be polished regularly with copper cleaner or—here is a trade secret—ketchup. Really!

earthenware

This material is not commonly used because it is not as strong as metal and is not a good heat conductor, therefore not good for stove-top use.

enameled cast iron

A very smart choice for a soup pot, marmite, or Dutch oven is enameled cast iron. Dishes that are cooked on a low temperature for a long time are best served with enameled cast iron. Select a burner that closely matches the width of the pan to prevent energy loss. Use only wooden, plastic, or heat-resistant utensils to avoid scratching the interior. If you are going to invest in enameled cast iron, which can be costly, you must also invest in a trivet. The pot will stay hot for a while, so once you are finished cooking, set the pot on the trivet to stop the cooking and cool the pot evenly. To clean, allow the pot or pan to cool completely and wash in hot soapy water. You may soak it briefly to loosen any food sticking to the pan and, if necessary, use a nylon scrubber. Dry immediately after washing; do not let a wet pot sit in a drying rack or water spots may appear.

glass, glass and ceramic, and porcelain

Although not very good heat conductors, these materials have many uses. The best aspect is that the glass and ceramic combination allows you to make a dish and freeze it, then pull it out to defrost in the refrigerator, then cook it and take it straight to the table. Be careful about sudden temperature changes though. Allow the pot, pan, or casserole dish to cool before putting water in it. All of these are nonreactive and safe for the dishwasher.

stainless steel

Even though many pans are called stainless steel, not many companies offer plain stainless-steel pots and pans. Although it is nonreactive, strong, and attractive, stainless steel has poor heat conductivity. More common is clad stainless steel (see above).

When choosing cookware, quality should be your first concern. This does not necessarily mean that the pan will be expensive. A very good cast-iron grill pan, for example, doesn't cost more than the price of a couple of tickets to the movies. You can start your

 **sorting it out**

collection with a few pans or the ten-piece set you received as a wedding gift. You will probably want to start with pots and pans that have many uses, such as fry pans and saucepans. Gradually, you can add more specialized kitchen tools, like a crêpe pan, which is essential for making the delicate French pancakes, and a braiser with its dome-shaped lid, which increases condensation, making it the perfect pot for cooking with moist heat.

a good, basic collection		
1-quart saucepan	10-inch nonstick fry pan	6-quart soup pot with lid
3-quart saucepan with lid	12-inch cast-iron sauté pan	Steamer insert
Grill pan	4-quart round Dutch oven	Wok

bouillabaisse pot, dutch oven, and marmite

Dutch ovens are large, deep pots that allow you to brown food on the stove top and then finish the dish either on the stove top or in the oven, which makes them ideal for stews. They are round or oval and are typically made of enameled cast iron, which slow-stews from the bottom and sides of the pot for even cooking. A bouillabaisse pot, or marmite, is a variation on a Dutch oven and has sloping sides. It is intended for soups and stews, including the classic French fish stew, bouillabaisse. Always use medium-low or low heat when cooking with these pots so the flavors have time to develop.

braiser

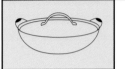

The tight-fitting, domed lid is the key element of this tool, designed for the type of slow cooking called braising. The lid collects the condensed steam created during cooking and returns it to the food, so that after the meat is browned, any liquid added will not evaporate as the dish cooks over a low flame. I recommend one about 13 inches wide, but I have also seen petit braisers that are only 10 inches across. They are available in clad stainless steel, anodized aluminum, and enameled cast iron.

crêpe pan

This oval or round pan, which originated in France, has just a tiny lip around the edge. The flat but limited surface enables the cook to make paper-thin crêpes, or pancakes, which is nearly impossible to do on a much larger griddle. A crêpe pan is normally about 8 inches in diameter and is available in clad stainless steel, nonstick, and copper.

double boiler

A double boiler allows you to cook delicate foods like chocolate or custard over simmering water, instead of over direct heat. It consists of two pots, one nesting snugly in the other, and a lid. The bottom pot holds the simmering water and sits directly over the heat while the top pot contains the food. The top and bottom of most double boilers normally hold about 3 quarts each. These pots are available in clad stainless steel, anodized aluminum, and copper.

fish poacher

The fish poacher, a French invention, effortlessly delivers the most delicate fish you will ever have. The oval or rectangular pan is normally about 12 to 14 inches long, comes with a lid, and has a perforated insert or rack. Add about 3 inches of seasoned water to the pan and then place a whole fish or fillets on the rack and lower them into the bath. Fish poachers are available in clad stainless steel, anodized aluminum, and copper.

fondue pot

This versatile stove-to-table pot is designed for dishes called fondue, which involve dipping foods directly into the pot. Bread and vegetables are dipped in melted cheese fondue, fruit is dipped in melted chocolate, and bits of meat are actually cooked in sizzling oil. Although stainless-steel pots are available, they are not very good for starting a fondue on the stove or for oil-pot fondues, because they do not distribute the heat evenly. Enameled cast iron or clad stainless steel are the optimum choices, because they retain heat well, allowing you to cook on a very low flame so the fondue will not burn on the bottom of the pot. A fondue pot commonly comes on a stand with a place for sterno underneath to keep the contents warm at the table.

fry pan

This is one of the most common pans in the modern kitchen. The sloping sides of this round pan, also called a skillet, insure that steam will not collect in the pan. It is available in clad stainless steel, nonstick, cast iron, copper, and enameled cast iron, in a range of sizes, most often between 8 and 12 inches in diameter.

gratin pan

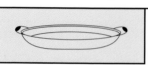

This round or oval ovenproof pan is shallow and has handles on both sides. It is designed for gratin recipes, which are topped with cheese or breadcrumbs, dotted with butter, and then baked in the oven and finished under the broiler. The shallow pan ensures that each portion will have a crispy top. Gratin pans are available in several sizes, from about 8 to 14 inches, and come in clad stainless steel, glass, porcelain, copper, earthenware, and enameled cast iron.

griddle

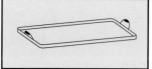

Griddles are commonly made of thick, heavy metals that are good heat conductors, such as cast iron. A single-burner griddle often has a long handle, while the double-burner griddle has a looped handle on either end. The griddle may have a very low rim and some manufacturers have cleverly designed a two-sided griddle/grill pan. Very little oil or clarified butter is needed for this tool once it is properly seasoned.

grill pan

The ridges of this stove-top phenomenon are what enable you to grill meat, fish, or vegetables to perfection indoors, without oil, anytime. The ridges sear the food while the valleys collect steam, insuring perfectly grilled foods. Grill pans are available in square, round, and oval sizes, and there are large, rectangular double-burner models as well. Choose one made of clad stainless steel, anodized aluminum, or enameled cast iron with a non-stick or stick-resistant interior, or season a cast-iron grill pan.

moroccan tagine

This two-piece pot with an unusual shape is specifically designed for a classic North African stew of the same name. Made from cast iron or porcelain-enameled cast iron, the pot has shallow sides and a conical lid. A tagine can be made with poultry or meat that is gently simmered with vegetables, olives, and spices and then served at the table right from the pot.

omelet pan

Named for the egg dish, the omelet pan has shallow, sloping sides, a flat bottom, and a long handle to enable you to easily turn and remove the delicate package without breaking it. Ranging in sizes from 6 to 12 inches in diameter, omelet pans are available in clad stainless steel and anodized aluminum with a nonstick interior and enameled cast iron.

paella pan

Paella is a Spanish dish made with saffron-laced rice and a variety of meats and shellfish. Although it is an old classic, it has gained popularity lately. So has the tool of the same name that is designed for it—a shallow loop-handled pan, normally about 13 inches in diameter. It is available in clad stainless steel and hand-hammered carbon steel. Paella is traditionally served from the pan at the table.

pasta pentola

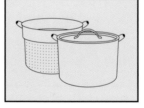

What a marvelous invention! The pentola, which means pot or pan in Italian, comes with a colander insert that slips out so you can easily drain foods like pasta or boiled potatoes. Without the insert, it also doubles as a soup pot. It is typically 4 to 5 quarts and is available in clad stainless steel and anodized aluminum.

saucepan

A saucepan is often the first or second pan anyone adds to his or her kitchen. Deeper than a sauté pan, it comes with a long handle and a tight-fitting lid and is available in a range of sizes: small (1 pint to 2 quarts), medium (3 and 4 quarts), and large (5 and 6 quarts). These pans are always very well balanced and are made from a variety of materials, including clad stainless steel, anodized aluminum, glass, copper, and enameled cast iron.

saucier

This is a specially designed pan similar in appearance to a saucepan, but with curved sides that allow you to easily use a whisk while making sauces. It is traditionally about 4 quarts and made of clad stainless steel or copper.

sauté pan

This essential straight-sided pan is available in medium (2 to 4 quarts) and large (5 to 7 quarts) sizes and comes with a long handle and lid. Deeper than a fry pan, but shallow enough for sautéing with ease, it is perfect for browning meat and then simmering it in a sauce. It is usually made of clad stainless steel, anodized aluminum, or cast iron.

steamer

There are two styles on the market: One is an Asian bamboo steamer, which consists of one or more slatted stackable trays, for different layers of foods, and a lid. Often it is set inside a wok. The other is a steamer insert used in conjunction with a saucepan and most commonly made of clad stainless steel or anodized aluminum.

stir-fry pan or chef's pan

This is a modern hybrid of the wok and fry pan. It is a little easier to use than a wok because of the long handle on one side, the looped handle on the other, and the flat bottom. The stir-fry pan is my first choice when making risotto because I can easily get under the rice to stir it constantly. This pan is usually 10 or 12 inches in diameter and is made of clad stainless steel or anodized aluminum.

stockpot and soup pot

These are tall-sided pots with tight-fitting lids and loop handles on either side. They range from 4 quarts all the way to twenty. While many manufacturers call them all stockpots, I refer to the smaller ones (4 to 6 quarts) as soup pots. Commonly made of clad stainless steel, anodized aluminum, and copper, they are good for slow cooking over medium-low heat. Because the sides are tall and relatively small in diameter, stocks and soups do not evaporate quickly.

wok

This popular, ancient cooking utensil is ideal for stir-frying, steaming, and even deep-frying over high heat. The high flared sides of this wide pan radiate the heat and give you plenty of room to cook your food, which conveniently falls back into the bottom of the pot during stir-frying. It is typically a round-bottomed wide pan made of rolled steel that must be seasoned, but today's manufacturers offer it in clad stainless steel, anodized aluminum, and hand-hammered steel as well. It has a loop handle on either side and customarily comes with a cylindrical base for cooking over a gas flame.

Below is a glossary of techniques you will encounter as you cook your way from Authentic Crêpes to silky Zabaglione and Berries. With some practice you will be surprised how good you become at making dishes you have only tried in restaurants, such as blackened steak and poached fish.

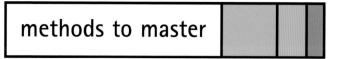

methods to master

blackening

Only a cast-iron fry pan can be used to authentically create this delicious Cajun style of cooking from New Orleans, because it can take the heat without any damage to the pan. The flavor comes from the seasoning, which is rubbed on fish, chicken, or beef. Then the food is cooked in a dry, red-hot pan until it is blackened and crusty. You must have good ventilation or an outside burner for this technique because the pan will smoke when you add the raw food. Also, be careful—this is high-temperature cooking—but do try it at home.

boiling and simmering

Everyone can boil water. When I meet people who tell me they cannot cook, I simply ask if they can fill a pot with water and turn on the burner. When the liquid reaches 212°F (at sea level), bubbles will break the surface. And voilà—you're cooking! A simmer produces small bubbles and a rapid boil creates large ones. When simmering, be gentle—very gentle. The liquid should be just below a boil—hot enough so tiny bubbles delicately cook the food. This is not a quick cooking method. Simmered dishes develop flavor with great care.

braising and stewing

One of my favorites! Meat or vegetables are first browned in the pan with a bit of fat to improve flavor and appearance. It almost feels as if you are burning the meat or vegetables, but as long as you keep your heat on medium and have patience, you will succeed. Once the meat or vegetables are browned, liquid is added and the pan is tightly covered. The food cooks slowly on a low heat, which develops the flavor. This technique will not work in a pan with a nonstick surface because it does not allow you to brown the foods properly.

broiling and grilling

This direct-heat cooking method is volatile and food can quickly become overdone! Most of you are familiar with the broiling opportunity your oven offers, either in the oven or in the broiling drawer. Make sure to preheat the broiler before adding the food. Grilling is a form of broiling, with heat below rather than above. Never leave the scene—keep a close eye on broiling and grilling.

deglazing

This technique revives the pan and collects the flavor after ingredients are browned. Either wine or stock is the liquid of choice, although water also works. Once the meat or vegetables are browned, the liquid is added and the bits are scraped up from the bottom. Now you have the flavor base for a braised dish, stew, or soup. Avoid pans with a nonstick coating when deglazing, as they don't form as much of the browned flavorful bits.

frying

Don't be afraid of deep-frying. Just make sure the oil is hot enough, usually 350°F to 375°F, and your food will turn out wonderfully crisp on the outside and juicy on the inside. Invest in a deep-fat thermometer to keep in tune with your oil temperature. Do not ever crowd your pan when you are deep-frying. If it has been deep-fried properly, the food should not drain off a lot of oil when transferred to a paper towel. The type of oil is important, too. The oils best for deep-frying can take a lot of heat without smoking—peanut oil is at the top of the list. Some dishes such as Keep It Coming Tempura are better deep-fried in vegetable oil or even the old-fashioned vegetable shortening, as with 'Tucky Fried Chicken.

poaching

Do not be too intimidated to learn how to poach, which is simply cooking food in liquid. The secret is the temperature of the poaching liquid, which must be at a simmer and covering the ingredients just halfway. Vegetables, fish, and chicken can all be poached to perfection either in a fancy poacher or in a large skillet. Once you learn this technique and various seasonings for flavoring the cooking liquid, beautiful poached dishes will liven up your culinary repertoire. Because the food is not browned before adding the liquid, poaching can be a very low-fat technique.

roasting

Start with a tender piece of meat, place it in a pan with vegetables, put it in the oven, uncovered, and you are roasting. It is that simple. A well-browned exterior with a moist, juicy interior is what you want from using this method of dry, indirect heat. As always, temperature is crucial because too hot and the outside of the food burns, too low and it dries out. Preheat your oven and watch your timing.

sautéing and stir-frying

This is a delicate form of frying, using little oil and cooking quickly over high heat. Almost anything can be sautéed, although different foods should be of similar sizes to promote even cooking. Practice the "sauté flip" by jerking the pan forward and then back again, and you will be an expert. The quick toss is done without a utensil, insuring that whatever you are cooking does not break up. Pan-frying sometimes uses more oil than sautéing, but is essentially the same.

steaming

During the past couple of decades, steaming has become ever more popular in the United States because it needs no fat, but it has been a common method of cooking in other parts of the world for centuries. A metal insert or bamboo steamer is placed over a pot of simmering water, the food is placed in the steamer, and the pot is covered. With the proper seasoning, steaming is a flavorful, fat-free, healthy option that anyone can do with ease.

Almost everyone likes a leisurely brunch or lunch. Eggs are an important ingredient in many brunch dishes, so treat them properly by taking them out of the refrigerator in time for them to warm up a bit. Afternoon sports offer a great opportunity to enjoy lunch with friends, so I have included some recipes for those special get-togethers, such as *Laguna Fish Tacos* and *Halftime Chili*. Your griddle will be your partner to make old favorites from *Famously French Toast* to *Classic Grilled Cheese*. I have also included stove-to-table meals that are always welcome any time for easy cleanup.

delicious anytime

The batter for these delicate French pancakes must be chilled before you use it. The crêpes can be made in advance and saved between sheets of wax paper at room temperature for up to three hours. If you are not going to use them the same day, they can be stored in the refrigerator in a sealed container for up to three days. I recommend using ghee (the Hindi word for clarified butter), to cook the crêpes. It has a higher smoke point than regular butter because the milk solids, which burn easily, have been removed. Ghee can be found in most gourmet stores and all Indian food markets. ☐ A **crêpe pan** is the only tool that will enable you to master perfectly thin, light golden brown crêpes. The pan has low sides and is about 8 inches in diameter, so the batter for one crêpe can spread across the entire pan. Learning how to use the crêpe pan is not that difficult once you practice a couple of times. The secret is to add just the right amount of batter to the hot pan and then spread it out by lifting the pan and rotating it from side to side quickly to coat the inside of the pan evenly, taking care not to let the batter drip off the sides.

authentic crêpes

¾ **cup sifted unbleached all-purpose flour**

1½ **teaspoons sugar**

½ **teaspoon kosher salt**

3 **large eggs, at room temperature**

1½ **cups whole milk**

2 **tablespoons clarified butter (ghee)**

serves 4 to 6; makes about 12 crêpes

Combine the flour, sugar, and salt in a bowl. Put the eggs in a blender and blend just until the whites and yolk are combined. Add the flour mixture to the eggs and blend just until smooth. Add milk and blend again just until smooth. Cover the blender and refrigerate the batter for at least 1 hour and no more than 3 hours. The batter will thicken as it stands. When you are ready to make the crêpes, remix the batter in the blender for about 30 seconds.

If necessary, heat the butter in a small glass bowl in the microwave on high until it liquefies, about 30 seconds. Using a pastry brush, wipe a crêpe pan with a little of the butter and warm over medium heat until hot. Add about

continued

2 tablespoons of the batter and tilt the pan so the batter evenly coats the pan in a thin layer. Cook for about 1 minute. The crêpe will easily lift off the pan as you turn it over with a small spatula. Cook on the other side for 1 minute more. Slide the cooked crêpe onto a platter lined with wax paper. Using a pastry brush, coat the pan with more butter and repeat until all the batter is used, separating the crêpes with wax paper. Place a linen kitchen towel over the platter of cooked crêpes until you are done cooking.

About half an hour before you are ready to serve, preheat the oven to 350°F. Fill each crêpe with about 2 tablespoons of anything that suits your fancy, such as fruit compotes, fresh strawberries, or savory fillings like creamed spinach, sautéed mushrooms, or chicken and cheese. Roll the crêpes up like a burrito over the filling and place in a baking pan. Heat for about 15 minutes. Remove the crêpes and serve on warm plates or set out the baking dish and people can help themselves.

Challah, a Jewish braided bread with a texture similar to a brioche, was the hands-down winner when I tested this recipe. Have fun with the toppings and use only pure maple syrup. Depending on your personal preference, you can use ghee (the Hindi word for clarified butter) or bacon fat to fry the toast. The toast can be made ahead and kept warm in the oven. Do not stack the pieces directly on top of each other; a stair step stack works better so the toast does not get soggy. □ A **griddle**, an essential pan for the well-equipped kitchen, works best here. Learning how to use this tool is mostly about heating it to the right temperature: not too hot, not too cold. The water test works best for me. When the pan is heated just enough, a sprinkle of water should pop, not smoke. Be sure to allow the griddle to heat up between batches. Then a light wipe of the ghee on the surface, and you are ready to make more. It is important to keep the griddle clean, so if you see bits of egg on the pan between batches, use a paper towel to collect them so they will not burn.

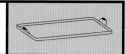

famously french toast

3 large eggs, at room temperature

¾ cup whole milk

2 teaspoons sugar

2 tablespoons clarified butter (ghee) or bacon fat

Eight 1-inch slices challah bread

Pure maple syrup for serving

2 tablespoons powdered sugar

serves 4

Preheat the oven to 200°F and place a heatproof platter inside. In a wide shallow bowl, beat the eggs until very well blended. Add the milk and then the granulated sugar, blending very well. Heat a griddle over medium heat until water dances when sprinkled on it. Using a pastry brush, coat the griddle evenly with the butter. Briefly soak a slice of bread on each side in the egg mixture and place on the griddle. Cook for about 2 minutes, turn over with a spatula, and cook for 2 minutes more. Transfer the toast to the platter in the oven and repeat until all of the toast has been cooked. Heat the syrup in a saucepan or the microwave. Place the toast on serving plates, sprinkle with the powdered sugar, and serve immediately with the warm syrup.

According to legend, regular patrons Mr. and Mrs. LeGrand Benedict came up with this dish to relieve their boredom with the lunch menu at Delmonico's in New York. It is still a favorite on almost every brunch menu in America. Follow the hash browns recipe precisely, and you will be able to make them with ease. Use a large clad stainless steel **saucepan** to boil the potatoes—they need plenty of room to keep their shape. A medium nonstick **fry pan** is essential because you will need to

legrand eggs benedict and diner hash browns

DINER HASH BROWNS

4 russet potatoes
(about 1½ pounds total)

2 teaspoons kosher salt, divided

¼ cup olive oil

3 tablespoons unsalted butter,
divided

2 large sweet onions,
cut into ½-inch dice

¼ teaspoon freshly ground pepper

**TIME-HONORED
HOLLANDAISE SAUCE**
makes about 1 cup

½ cup (1 stick) unsalted butter

1 tablespoon fresh lemon juice,
plus extra to taste

1 tablespoon water

¼ teaspoon kosher salt

3 large egg yolks

invert the pan to flip the potatoes, and it will work well for the bacon too. The pan should have a metal or heat-resistant handle so it can go into the oven, allowing you to keep the hash browns warm while you poach the eggs. ☐ Keep your hollandaise sauce warm in the top of a **double boiler**—if it gets cold, it cannot be reheated. A double boiler is designed for heat-sensitive foods, such as the fussy but delicious hollandaise sauce. If you have a copper double boiler, it will make the sauce extra creamy. Learn how to keep the water in the bottom at a very slow simmer. Use the saucepan to poach the eggs, and remove them with a large slotted spoon. The water should be at a slow boil so the bubbles will not break up the eggs.

serves 4

To make the hash browns: Peel the potatoes and cut them into ½-inch cubes. You should have about 3 cups. Put the potatoes in a large saucepan and fill it with enough water to cover the potatoes. Add 1½ teaspoons of the salt and bring to a gentle boil over medium heat. Cover with a lid slightly askew and boil for about 5 minutes or until they are just soft enough to pierce easily with a knife. Drain the potatoes in a colander and set aside.

In a medium nonstick fry pan, heat the oil and 1 tablespoon of the butter over medium heat until hot but not smoking. Add the onions and remaining ½ teaspoon salt to the pan and sauté, stirring occasionally, until the onions are soft and caramelized. Add the potatoes and pepper and toss to coat them well with the onion mixture. Using a spatula, press the potatoes down in the fry pan to form a cake. Cook until crispy on the bottom, about 10 minutes.

Place a plate or a baking sheet without sides over the fry pan and carefully invert the potato cake onto it. Add the remaining 2 tablespoons butter to the fry pan and melt over medium heat. Carefully slide the potato cake back into the fry pan and cook for 10 minutes more. Serve immediately or return to the baking sheet to keep warm in the oven.

To make the hollandaise: Fill the bottom of a double boiler halfway (about 3 inches) with water and bring to a low simmer over medium-low heat. Cut the butter into 4 pieces and set aside. Add the juice, water, and salt to the top of the double boiler and heat to lukewarm. Make sure that steam from the lower part of the double boiler does not get into the top where the sauce is. The water should never come to a full boil. Add the eggs to the lemon mixture and use a whisk to beat constantly until thickened. Add one fourth of the butter, whisking steadily until blended thoroughly. Repeat with the remaining butter. Remove the pan from the heat and stir in a few additional drops of lemon juice to taste, if desired. Keep the pan covered in a warm place, but do not reheat!

To make the eggs: Fill a large saucepan halfway with water and add the vinegar. Heat over medium heat until the water is simmering. At the same time, heat a

EGGS BENEDICT

- 1 tablespoon distilled white vinegar
- 2 tablespoons unsalted butter
- 8 slices Canadian bacon
- 8 large eggs, at room temperature
- 4 English muffins, split and well toasted
- 2 tablespoons chopped fresh parsley

continued

medium fry pan over medium heat until hot. Add the butter to the fry pan and cook the Canadian bacon for about 2 minutes on each side to brown. Reduce the heat to low.

Crack the eggs, one at a time, into a small bowl and gently slip 2 of the eggs into the simmering water. Use a slotted spoon to gently keep the whites intact as best as you can. Poach the eggs for 3 to 5 minutes, until they are cooked to your liking. Gently remove the eggs, one at a time, with the slotted spoon and allow the water to drain off. Place each egg on top of a slice of Canadian bacon resting in the fry pan and then repeat with the remaining eggs. While you are poaching the eggs, transfer 2 of the English muffins to each of 4 warm plates. Transfer each slice of egg-topped Canadian bacon to an English muffin half. Spoon some hollandaise sauce over each egg and sprinkle with parsley. Serve immediately with the hash browns.

A frittata is an Italian omelet that has the filling incorporated into the eggs rather than folded inside. It is the absolute perfect choice for brunch or lunch. Serve with toast or biscuits and a salad to complete the meal. The basic technique for this popular dish is so simple that Sunday morning frittatas may soon become a custom in your home. First sauté a basic flavor base of onions, peppers, or meat. Then add eggs and anything else you like and enjoy your own signature style. ☐ It is important to use a nonstick **fry pan** so the frittata slides out easily. The size of the pan is dependent on the number of servings you need. Increase the size of the pan and the number of eggs for more people. To serve 4 people, use 8 eggs and a medium pan. To serve 6 people, use 12 eggs and a large pan. Most fry pans do not come with lids, so borrow one from another pan. It doesn't need to be tight fitting, just large enough to trap the steam, so the eggs will rise.

freestyle frittata

2 tablespoons olive oil

1/2 cup chopped scallions
(white parts only)

2 garlic cloves, crushed

1/2 red bell pepper, seeded
and diced

1/2 yellow bell pepper, seeded
and diced

1/2 Anaheim chile, seeded
and diced

1 small zucchini, diced

1 small yellow crookneck squash,
diced

8 large eggs, beaten

2 tablespoons whole milk

1/2 teaspoon kosher salt

1/4 teaspoon baking powder

1/4 teaspoon freshly ground pepper

1 cup (4 ounces) grated Gruyère
cheese

serves 4

Preheat the broiler. Heat a medium nonstick fry pan over medium heat and add the oil. Add the scallions and sauté for 2 minutes, until soft. Add the garlic and sauté for 1 minute more. Add the peppers and chile. Sauté for 2 minutes. Add the squashes and sauté for 1 minute. Meanwhile, put the eggs in a medium bowl and add the milk, salt, baking powder, and pepper. Whisk briefly to blend well. Using a spoon, arrange the vegetables evenly over the bottom of the fry pan. Slowly pour the egg mixture into the pan, being careful not to disturb the vegetables too much. Sprinkle the cheese on top of the frittata.

Reduce the heat to low and cover the pan. Steam the frittata for 10 to 12 minutes, or until set. Remove the lid and place the fry pan under broiler until the top is golden, about 2 minutes. Carefully slide the frittata onto a serving plate and slice into wedges. Serve immediately.

Everyone loves flapjacks, period. These "griddle-baked" cakes have been a breakfast favorite since the 1600s. Ghee, or clarified butter, is available at most gourmet markets and all Indian food markets. It has a higher smoke point than butter because the milk solids, which burn easily, have been removed. The syrup is best heated. I like to use a glass Pyrex measuring cup and briefly heat the syrup in the microwave. ☐ A **griddle** is wonderful for flapjacks because there are no sides to get in the way of flipping them. A well-seasoned cast-iron griddle will require very little butter. Or use a nonstick griddle, since those available today are far superior to those of yesteryear. It must be the perfect temperature, though. Drops of water should "dance" on the griddle when it's ready. You will also need a couple of mixing bowls for this recipe.

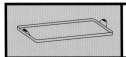

fearless flapjacks

1 cup unbleached all-purpose flour

2 teaspoons sugar

½ teaspoon kosher salt

½ teaspoon baking powder

¼ teaspoon baking soda

1 cup buttermilk

2 tablespoons whole milk

1 large egg, separated

2 tablespoons clarified butter (ghee), plus extra for brushing the griddle

Pure maple syrup

serves 4

In a large bowl, whisk together the flour, sugar, salt, baking powder, and baking soda. In medium bowl, combine the buttermilk and milk. Whisk the egg white into the milk mixture. Heat a griddle over medium-low heat and the oven to 200°F. Meanwhile, add the egg yolk to the butter. Add the milk mixture and the butter mixture to the dry ingredients and whisk just until combined. Do not overbeat the batter.

Test the heat of the griddle with a few drops of water. If the water "dances" on the surface, you are ready to make flapjacks. Using a paper towel or pastry brush, lightly coat the griddle with butter. Using a ladle, pour about ¼ cup of batter onto the griddle to make each flapjack, positioning them about 2 inches apart. When the tops of the flapjacks start to bubble after 2 to 3 minutes, use a spatula to gently flip them over and cook for 2 minutes more, until browned.

Transfer the flapjacks to a serving platter in the oven, grease the griddle, and repeat until all the batter is cooked. Serve with warm maple syrup.

My mummy, Janeé, has a few recipes that I crave to this day. She whips up a mixture of fat and flour, which is essentially a roux, to make these yummy patties. ☐ A medium **saucier** works best for the roux. Then a large cast-iron **fry pan** is my first choice for making the croquettes, because

struttin' salmon croquettes

it conducts heat so well and will give them a good crust. You can use a nonstick fry pan if you do not have a cast-iron one yet. But trust me, you really do need one.

serves 4; makes 8 patties

To make the sauce: In a glass or nonreactive metal bowl, whisk together the sour cream, mayonnaise, horseradish, herbs, and juice. Cover and refrigerate for at least 2 hours and no more than 24 hours.

To make the croquettes: Beat 1 egg well and set aside. Melt the butter in a medium saucier over medium-low heat. Whisk in the flour, then stir in the milk gradually. Cook for about 5 minutes, whisking constantly, or until thick and silky smooth. Remove from the heat and add the salmon, the beaten egg, and cracker crumbs. Mix thoroughly and chill for at least 2 hours and no more than 24 hours.

Form the salmon mixture into 2-inch patties about 1 inch thick. Beat the remaining 2 eggs in a shallow bowl. With your hands, break up the stuffing mix onto a plate so it resembles bread crumbs. Dip the patties in the egg and then roll in the stuffing mix, being careful to maintain the patty shapes. Heat the oil in a large fry pan over medium heat until hot but not smoking. Place the patties in the hot oil and fry for about 4 minutes on one side, or until golden brown. Gently turn and fry for about 3 minutes more, or until golden brown. Transfer to paper towels to drain. Serve with the Horseradish Sauce.

HORSERADISH DIPPING SAUCE
makes about 1 cup

¾ cup sour cream

¼ cup mayonnaise

2 tablespoons prepared white horseradish

2 tablespoons chopped fresh dill, tarragon, or basil

1 tablespoon fresh lemon juice

SALMON CROQUETTES

3 large eggs, divided

2 tablespoons unsalted butter

5 tablespoons unbleached all-purpose flour

½ cup whole milk

One 8-ounce can salmon, picked over for bones and flaked

⅓ cup Saltine cracker crumbs

1 cup Pepperidge Farm Stuffing Mix

2 tablespoons canola oil

I talked to several chef friends of mine about the mystique of the perfect omelet and how to achieve it. Thus, I tested two distinct methods of blending the eggs and found that both work very well. I have given directions for the simpler of the two below. If you want an even fluffier omelet and are not feeling rushed, separate the yolks and whites. Beat the whites until they will hold soft peaks, then gently fold them into the beaten yolks before cooking. You can fill your omelet with almost anything, such as cheese, cooked meats, and vegetables. This recipe can be doubled to infinity. ☐ Here's the perfect time to use a beautiful copper bowl. When you whisk the eggs in it, they'll become fluffy and light. The French developed the **omelet pan** with its sloping sides, which make it simple to slide out the omelet. If you do not have one, a small nonstick fry pan will do the job. Do not let the pan become too hot before adding the eggs, and tend to the eggs with care. You do not want to simply add the eggs and let them sit; they need to be stirred around a bit in the pan. I like to use a small, heat-resistant spatula for the job.

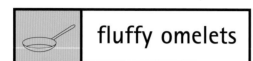

fluffy omelets

2 large eggs

¹/₄ teaspoon kosher salt

¹/₄ teaspoon freshly ground pepper

1 teaspoon unsalted butter

3 tablespoons grated cheese

1¹/₂ teaspoons snipped fresh chives

serves 1; makes 1 omelet

Put the eggs in a small copper or other bowl, add the salt and pepper, and whisk well. Heat an omelet pan over medium heat until hot, and add the butter. Tilt the pan as the butter melts, to coat the entire bottom of the pan. Slowly pour the beaten eggs into the pan. Using a small spatula, gently stir the center of the eggs without breaking the edges. As the eggs begin to cook, slide the spatula under the edges of the omelet to release it from the pan. Sprinkle the cheese and chives over one side of the omelet. Once the eggs are no longer loose, use the spatula to gently fold the side without the filling onto the other one. Jiggle the pan to completely release the omelet, and slide it onto a warm plate to serve.

The better the cuts of meat you use, the better this chili, which calls for both beef and lamb. I do not put beans in this recipe, but if you like, you can add a 16-ounce can of red beans about 30 minutes before serving. The longer this cooks, the better it is. Cook it up to 3 days ahead, and allow the chili to cool completely. Then store it, covered, in the refrigerator and heat it up very slowly when you are ready to serve it. The flavors will have married to create a tasty rich dish. Chili can also be frozen in an airtight container for 1 month. ☐ A large enameled cast-iron **Dutch oven** is my choice for this crowd-pleaser. Simmering the meat is the most essential step, and the enameled cast-iron finish on the inside of the pot is perfect for the job.

halftime chili

serves 8 to 10

Heat the oil in a large heavy Dutch oven over medium-high heat. Add the sweet onions and salt. Sauté for 8 to 10 minutes, or until they are soft. Add the garlic and sauté for 2 minutes more. Add the beef and lamb, stirring very well. Sauté the meat until browned on all sides, about 10 minutes. Stir in the chili powder, cumin, oregano, basil, thyme, and pepper. Add the stock, crushed tomatoes, beer, and tomato paste. Bring mixture to a slow boil and then lower the heat to medium-low. Simmer the chili, uncovered, until thickened, stirring occasionally, for about 1 hour and 15 minutes.

To serve, ladle the chili into bowls and garnish with red onion, cheese, and cilantro.

2 tablespoons olive oil

2 medium sweet onions, chopped

1 teaspoon kosher salt

6 large garlic cloves, minced

2 pounds beef filet or beef chuck, cut into 1/4-inch pieces

1 pound boneless lamb, cut into 1/4-inch pieces

5 tablespoons chili powder

1 tablespoon ground cumin

1 teaspoon dried oregano

1 teaspoon dried basil

1/2 teaspoon dried thyme

1/2 teaspoon freshly ground pepper

4 cups Beefy Beef Stock (page 74) or good-quality low-sodium canned broth

One 28-ounce can crushed tomatoes

One 12-ounce bottle ale or lager beer

One 6-ounce can tomato paste

1/2 red onion, minced

2 cups (8 ounces) grated Cheddar cheese

1/4 cup chopped fresh cilantro

A place called Wahoo's serves these soft tacos in Laguna Beach, California, and they are so memorable some people visit the seaside village just to enjoy them. Firm white-fleshed fish such as sea bass or red snapper sauté perfectly for these delicious packages. ☐ A medium cast-iron **fry pan** works best for this dish because you can get it very hot to crisp the fish, but you can also use a medium nonstick fry pan. It is essential to heat the pan very well and cook the fish until it is almost done before turning it, so that it gets a nice crust, which will keep it light and moist. Resist the urge to disturb the fillet as it cooks on the first side so it will not stick.

laguna fish tacos

Eight 7-inch flour tortillas

1½ pounds skinless, firm, white-fleshed fish fillets, such as sea bass, snapper, or halibut, about ½ inch thick

1 tablespoon unsalted butter, melted

1 tablespoon canola oil

½ teaspoon kosher salt

¼ teaspoon freshly ground pepper

1 cup shredded iceberg lettuce

1 cup chopped plum tomatoes

½ cup sour cream

1 tablespoon fresh lime juice

serves 4

Preheat the oven to 200°F. Wrap the tortillas in aluminum foil and put them in the oven to warm.

Rinse and dry the fish fillets. Combine the butter and oil. Heat a medium fry pan over medium-high heat until very hot. Using a pastry brush, coat the fish with the butter and oil mixture and generously salt and pepper each fillet. Place in the preheated fry pan, flat sides up. Cook the fillets for 5 minutes without disturbing them. Shake the pan a little to make sure the fillets are ready to turn; they should move easily within the pan. Using a spatula, gently turn the fillets, reduce the heat to medium, and cook for 3 minutes more, until they are just cooked through. Transfer the fish fillets to a plate lined with paper towels to drain. Cut the fish into big chunks.

Assemble the tacos by adding equal portions of fish to each tortilla and then topping with the lettuce and tomato. Combine the sour cream and lime juice, drizzle a little on top of each taco, and serve immediately.

Serve this dish on its own with a salad or as a side dish for almost everything. You can try a mix of different cheeses and add other ingredients, such as peppers or meats, for different flavors. I like to use a bold cheese with a slightly nutty flavor.

☐ The **pasta pentola,** which I recommend for cooking the macaroni, is fairly new to the market. Making any pasta in this unique design is so much easier than the old-fashioned way of carrying a heavy pot of boiling water to the sink and dumping it into a colander.

mod mac and cheese

Once the pasta is cooked, simply lift the insert and tilt it to drain the water right back into the pot. You will need a medium **saucepan** to make the topping. Use very low heat; you do not want to cook the cheese, just warm it. A clad stainless steel or cast-iron **gratin pan** is perfectly suited for this dish because it can withstand the direct heat of the stove top and move right to the oven. It is wide and shallow, so everyone can have a bit of the crunchy top.

serves 4

Preheat the oven to 375°F. Fill a pasta pentola three quarters full of water and bring to a boil over medium heat.

Meanwhile, make the topping: Melt the butter over medium heat in a medium saucepan. Allow to cool slightly, and then add the breadcrumbs, tossing them in the butter with a fork. Add the cheese and toss again very lightly. The mixture should be fluffy.

Add 1 tablespoon of the salt to the boiling pasta water. Cook the pasta according to the package instructions and drain by lifting up the insert and tilting it. Rinse the pasta with water, toss with ½ tablespoon of the butter, and set aside.

TOPPING

- 2 tablespoons unsalted butter
- 2 cups coarse breadcrumbs
- 1 cup (4 ounces) grated Gruyère cheese

- 1 tablespoon plus ½ teaspoon kosher salt, divided
- 1 pound good-quality macaroni
- 1½ tablespoons unsalted butter
- 1 cup minced sweet onion
- 8 ounces prosciutto, chopped
- 1 cup heavy (whipping) cream
- ½ cup half-and-half
- ¼ teaspoon freshly ground pepper
- 2½ cups (12 ounces) sharp white Cheddar cheese

Wipe the inside of a gratin pan with some of the remaining 1 tablespoon butter and melt the rest in the gratin pan over low heat. Add the onion and remaining ½ teaspoon salt.

Sauté for about 5 minutes, until the onions are soft. Add the prosciutto and sauté for 2 minutes more. Add the cream, half-and-half, and pepper and scrape up any bits from the bottom of the pan. Add the macaroni and toss to coat well, then fold in the cheese. Cover the macaroni mixture with the topping and bake for 30 minutes. It should be golden brown and bubbling hot. Carefully remove the pan from the oven and allow the dish to rest for 15 minutes before serving.

Take your time when you make this classic Italian dish, and each time you add stock, only add enough to barely cover the rice. Risotto can be adapted to seasonal ingredients. The rice can be enhanced with flavorful cured meats, vegetables, and even fruit. Here I give you the basic recipe and technique along with three variations. The stock can also vary; use beef, chicken, or vegetable, depending on your taste. One ingredient that does not vary is the Arborio rice, a fat, starchy grain that gives risotto its creamy texture. You will find it at well-stocked supermarkets. □ A wide-bottomed pan enables the Arborio rice to cook evenly. A large sauté pan is fine, but I also like a **stir-fry pan.** The curved sides allow me to get under all of the rice with my stainless steel flat spoon, which is like a cross between a spoon and spatula. A clad stainless steel pan is the best choice because it heats so evenly.

right way risotto

5 to 6 cups Beefy Beef Stock (page 74) or Chicken Stock (page 76) or good-quality low-sodium canned broth

2 tablespoons olive oil

1 medium onion, diced

1 teaspoon kosher salt

2 garlic cloves, minced

2 cups Arborio rice

½ cup (4 ounces) grated Parmesan or Asiago cheese, plus extra for passing

2 tablespoons chopped fresh flat-leaf parsley or another fresh herb

serves 4 as a main course or 6 as a first course

In a medium saucepan, warm the stock over medium-low heat. Using a paper towel, wipe the interior of a stir-fry pan or large sauté pan with a little of the oil. Heat the pan over medium heat and add the remaining oil. Add the onion and salt and stir well. Sauté the onions for 3 to 5 minutes, or until soft. Add the garlic, stir well, and cook for 1 minute more. Add the rice and sauté for about 2 minutes, stirring frequently. The rice will start to look transparent, with a little seed inside. Using a ladle, add just enough stock to barely cover the rice. Stirring frequently, allow the rice to absorb the liquid. When it is almost gone, slowly add more stock until the rice is barely covered. Allow the rice to absorb most of the stock again and repeat until the rice is tender and creamy. This should take about 15 minutes. Stir in the cheese, mixing well. Serve immediately by spooning and spreading the risotto in a shallow layer on a platter. Garnish with fresh herbs and extra cheese.

variations

risotto primavera

I encourage you to get creative with different color combinations of vegetables. For the best presentation, cut the vegetables as close to the same size as you can.

Add ¼ cup diced bell pepper when you add the garlic. Cook as instructed, and add ¼ cup diced zucchini and ¼ cup diced mushrooms when half of the broth has been used. Continue with the recipe.

risotto con carne

I like using very flavorful meat for this variation, such as tasso—cured pork with Cajun seasoning available in finer gourmet markets. Although this is a meat variation, I use vegetable or chicken stock. The beef broth is a bit overpowering with the cured meat.

Add 4 ounces diced tasso, pancetta, or any other cured meat, when you add the garlic and add 1 minute to the sautéing time before adding the rice. Continue with the recipe.

risotto con funghi

Mushrooms, such as porcini, portobello, and chanterelle, offer such a deep flavor to risotto. I prefer beef stock with porcini and portobellos and vegetable stock with the chanterelles. You can also make up your own mushroom blends.

Add 2 cups chopped mushrooms when half of the broth has been used, and continue with the recipe.

Who can resist perfectly butter-toasted fragrant bread with hot, melting cheese inside? I prefer sourdough bread, but you can substitute good ol' American white bread if you like. Whole wheat or multigrain bread just doesn't get anyone I know excited about this. Serve it with True Tomato Soup (page 83). ☐ A perfectly heated **griddle** will insure crispy grilled cheese sandwiches. Don't allow the griddle to get too hot, or the butter will burn. Heat it just enough so water drops "dance" on the griddle, but do not smoke.

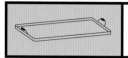

classic grilled cheese

4 slices Cheddar, American,
   or Swiss cheese

4 slices sourdough bread

4 tablespoons unsalted butter

serves 2

Preheat a griddle over medium heat until hot. Put 2 slices of cheese between 2 slices of bread to make 2 sandwiches. Melt 2 tablespoons of the butter on the griddle. When melted, add the sandwiches. Grill for 2 to 3 minutes, gently pressing down the sandwiches with a spatula once or twice during the grilling. When one side is golden, add the remaining 2 tablespoons of butter, turn the sandwiches over, and brown the other side, about 2 minutes more. Serve immediately.

variation

Add 3 slices of crispy bacon or ¼ cup diced ham or shredded chicken to each sandwich with the cheese and fry as directed.

M.A.N's chicken pot pie

This recipe came from my brother, Marc—M.A.N. are his initials—and his wife, Wendy. It is perfect for a weekend brunch because it is prepared in a cast-iron **fry pan,** so it can be assembled ahead of time and served right from the skillet.

serves 4

3 tablespoons unsalted butter, divided, plus extra for greasing

1 teaspoon kosher salt, divided

1/2 teaspoon freshly ground pepper, divided

1 pound 8 ounces skinless, boneless chicken breast halves

1/4 cup plus 2 tablespoons unbleached all-purpose flour

1 cup chopped celery

1 cup chopped carrot

1/2 cup chopped shallots

2 garlic cloves, minced

3 cups chicken stock (page 76) or good-quality low-sodium canned broth

1 1/2 cups diced russet potato

1 cup heavy (whipping) cream

8 sprigs fresh thyme

1 tablespoon chopped fresh flat-leaf parsley

2 bay leaves

1 cup frozen peas, thawed

One 10-ounce package frozen piecrust or pastry crust, thawed and refrigerated

1 large egg, lightly beaten with 1 1/2 teaspoons water

Preheat the oven to 375°F. Butter the inside of a medium fry pan and melt 2 tablespoons of the butter over medium heat. Meanwhile, using half of the salt and pepper, season the chicken. Put 1/4 cup of the flour into a shallow bowl and dredge each piece in flour to coat. Add the chicken pieces to the skillet and cook until just cooked through, about 5 minutes on the first side and 3 minutes more on the other side. Transfer to a platter to rest. Add the remaining 1 table-spoon butter to the hot skillet. Add the celery, carrot, and shallots and season with the remaining salt and pepper. Sauté for 5 minutes. Add the garlic and sauté for 1 minute more. Sprinkle the remaining 2 tablespoons flour into the fry pan, stir to mix well, and cook for about 2 minutes, or until the flour is absorbed. Add the stock, potato, cream, thyme, parsley, and bay leaves, bring to a simmer, and add the peas. Chop the chicken into bite-sized pieces and add to the pan. Remove from the heat and allow the mixture to rest for 15 minutes.

On a lightly floured surface, roll out the chilled dough into a circle slightly larger than the fry pan. Remove the bay leaves and thyme sprigs from the fry pan. Cover the fry pan with the dough and crimp the sides to seal. Make three 1-inch-long slits in the top of the crust near the center. Bake for 30 minutes. Brush the top of the crust with the egg wash and bake for 15 minutes more, or until the crust is golden. Remove from the oven and allow to rest for 15 minutes. To serve, scoop out portions onto warm plates.

Paella is a Spanish dish of saffron-flavored rice combined with a
variety of meats and shellfish. The recipe varies from one cook
to the next because you can make it with endless combina-
tions of ingredients. Here I include chicken, but I also like to use rabbit, and when I can get
them, frogs' legs! If you are lucky enough to get your hands on very fragrant, sweet, juicy,
naturally ripened tomatoes, by all means use them instead of the canned. Finally, this is a
dish you build. You add the stock to the rice gradually, as you do when making risotto. Take
your time. ☐ You will need a medium **saucepan** to heat the stock and keep it warm, so it
will not splatter when you add it to the paella pan. The **paella pan** is uniquely designed so
you can hold cooked food on the outer rim of the pan while you cook in the center. Then
you combine everything. I always serve paella by placing the pan in the middle of the table
and allowing my family and friends to help themselves. A big, flat, stainless steel spoon
works best for stirring.

plentiful paella

serves 6

Heat the stock, saffron, and bay leaf in a medium saucepan over low heat and
keep hot. Wipe the inside of a paella pan with a little oil and warm over medium
heat. Add the remaining oil and then the onion and ½ teaspoon of the salt.
Sauté for about 5 minutes, until the onion is soft. Add the peppers and garlic.
Cook for about 2 minutes. Push the mixture to the edges of the pan. Add
the sausages and cook, turning often, to brown on all sides, about 10 minutes.
Transfer the sausages and vegetables to a bowl to rest. While the sausages
are cooking, season the chicken with salt and pepper.

continued

5 cups Beefy Beef Stock (page 74),
Chicken Stock (page 76), or
good-quality low-sodium
canned broth

Generous pinch of saffron threads

1 bay leaf

1 tablespoon plus 1½ teaspoons
extra-virgin olive oil

1 large sweet onion, such as
Vidalia or Maui, chopped

1 teaspoon kosher salt, divided,
plus extra for seasoning

1 red bell pepper, seeded and cut
into ½-by-2-inch strips

1 yellow bell pepper, seeded and
cut into ½-by-2-inch strips

5 garlic cloves, chopped

1 pound good-quality spicy
sausages, such as Cajun or Italian

6 bone-in chicken thighs or one
2-pound rabbit, cut up, washed,
and patted dry

¼ teaspoon freshly ground pepper,
plus extra for seasoning

1 pound extra-large shrimp
(16–20), rinsed, deveined, tails
left on

1½ cups Arborio rice

One 8-ounce can chopped
tomatoes with juice

½ bunch fresh flat-leaf parsley,
chopped

Put the chicken in the empty paella pan and cook over medium heat for about 10 minutes on one side. Turn and cook for 5 to 6 minutes more, or until lightly browned and cooked through. Push the chicken to the edges of the pan. Add the shrimp and cook for 5 minutes on one side, turn, and cook for 3 minutes more. They should be slightly undercooked. Transfer the shrimp and the chicken to a platter and set aside.

Add the rice to the pan and stir very well as it begins to pop, about 3 minutes. Add the remaining ½ teaspoon of salt, the pepper, and tomatoes, stirring well. Slowly add about 1 cup of the warm stock to the rice and stir well. As the liquid is absorbed by the rice, add a little more, stirring frequently and getting underneath the rice thoroughly. When the rice is al dente, or firm to the tooth, cut the sausage into 1-inch slices and stir it into the rice, along with the onion mixture. Reduce the heat to low and then add the chicken. Add 1 more cup of stock and reheat the dish slowly. Then add the shrimp, evenly distributing them throughout the dish. The paella should be moist and slightly creamy. If it is too dry, add a little more stock. Sprinkle the parsley on top and serve immediately.

These days an entire party can start and finish with small bites, and at dinner parties, the appetizer course has become almost as important as the entrée. The recipes in this chapter tend to involve only one technique, giving you the opportunity to perfect a useful skill, such as sautéing the flavor base for *Smoky Avocado Relish and Crunchy Chips* in a nonstick fry pan, and stir-frying savory *Hot Woked Nuts* in your trusty wok. Most of the recipes are made in one pot and can be prepped in advance, so you can finish them off quickly when eager appetites are waiting and you want to join the fun!

bites to begin and party pleasures

A Northeast tradition, this dish is usually served piping hot with plenty of crusty bread to soak up the broth. Look for tightly closed clams when shopping. If the clam is slightly open, tap it lightly; if it does not snap shut, it's dead and should not be eaten. Littlenecks and cherrystone clams are my choice for this dish, but you can also use this same method for mussels. ☐ I recommend a clad stainless steel or anodized aluminum **stockpot** or large soup pot with a wide mouth, or a large sauté pan, so the clams have plenty of room to open and you can stir them easily.

surf's up steamers

2 tablespoons olive oil

½ cup minced shallots

2 teaspoons kosher salt

3 to 4 garlic cloves, minced

2½ cups dry white wine

2 bay leaves

4 pounds clams, scrubbed and rinsed well

4 tablespoons unsalted butter, cut into pieces

½ cup chopped fresh flat-leaf parsley

serves 4

Heat a stockpot or large soup pot over medium heat until hot. Add the oil, then the shallots and salt. Sauté for about 2 minutes, or until the shallots begin to soften. Add the garlic and sauté for 1 minute more. Add the wine and bay leaves and heat to a slow simmer. Cook for 3 minutes, then increase the heat to medium-high and add the clams. Cover and steam for 3 to 4 minutes. Stir well, cover again, and steam for 3 minutes more, or until the clams have opened. Do not overcook.

Using a large slotted spoon, transfer the clams to a serving bowl. Discard any clams that have not opened. Working quickly, add the butter to the stockpot and using a whisk, stir briskly until the butter is incorporated. Stir in the parsley and then pour the sauce over the clams. Serve immediately.

The secret to this relish is sautéing the flavor base before adding it to the avocado. The jalapeño pepper, scallions, and garlic need to "sweat" (pan steam) to develop their flavor. Most guacamole recipes do not instruct you to cook anything, but once you make it this way, you will appreciate the difference. I like to serve this with white corn tortilla chips. □ A

smoky avocado relish and crunchy chips

medium nonstick **fry pan** is best here so the flavor base stays moist and does not stick to the pan. You need a lid for this recipe. If your pan does not have one, borrow one from another pan.

4 ripe avocados

2 plum tomatoes, chopped

2 tablespoons minced fresh cilantro

1 tablespoon fresh lime juice

1 tablespoon plus 1 1/2 teaspoons olive oil

5 scallions (white parts only), minced

1/2 jalapeño pepper, seeded and minced

2 garlic cloves

1/2 teaspoon kosher salt

Crunchy chips for serving, such as white corn tortilla chips

serves 4

Peel and seed the avocados and place in a medium nonreactive metal or glass bowl. Add the tomatoes, cilantro, and juice. Using a spoon, mash the avocado into chunks as you mix it with the other ingredients.

Heat the oil in a medium nonstick fry pan over medium heat. Add the scallions and jalapeño. Using a garlic press, add the garlic to the pan. Add the salt and stir. Cover the pan and reduce the heat to low. Allow the mixture to cook for about 4 minutes without lifting the lid. The vegetables should be soft and fragrant. Remove the pan from the heat and allow to cool for about 5 minutes.

Lightly fold the scallion mixture into the avocado mixture, cover, and refrigerate for at least 30 minutes, but no more than 2 hours. Transfer the relish to a serving bowl and serve with chips.

I like to use fresh white summer corn when I make these. The sweet sugars in the corn kernels seem to explode when the fritters are cooked. Serve these yummy little treats with a crunchy salad and you have a perfect lunch! The secret to crispy corn fritters is keeping the oil hot. Make the fritters in batches, being careful not to crowd the pan. ☐ This recipe requires a deep, wide pot so that you can drop the spoonfuls of batter into the pan without splashing the oil. My favorite is a medium cast-iron **Dutch oven** with a strainer basket like the one made by Lodge (see Purveyors, page 140). As always, reheat the oil between batches.

crunchy corn fritters

serves 4 to 6

In a glass or nonreactive metal bowl, combine the flour, baking powder, and salt. Make a well in the center of the mixture. Break the eggs into the well. Stir the eggs with a fork, gradually mixing in the flour to form a batter. Stir in the corn and cilantro. Refrigerate the mixture for 15 minutes. Pour the oil into a medium Dutch oven to a depth of 4 inches. Clip a thermometer to the pan and heat the oil over medium-high heat to 375°F. Working in batches, carefully drop spoonfuls of the batter into the oil and cook until browned on both sides, about 2 minutes per side. Do not crowd the fritters. Using a spider strainer or strainer basket, remove the fritters and transfer them onto paper towels to drain. Reheat the oil and repeat until all the batter is used. Serve the fritters warm with maple syrup, salsa, or jam.

SPECIAL EQUIPMENT
spider strainer, deep-fat thermometer

½ **cup unbleached all-purpose flour**

½ **teaspoon baking powder**

½ **teaspoon kosher salt**

2 **large eggs**

2 **cups fresh corn kernels (from about 3 ears of corn)**

1 **tablespoon chopped fresh cilantro**

1½ **cups peanut oil for deep-frying**

Maple syrup, salsa, or jam for serving

Here is a party mix with a kick! The jalapeño peppers add a special punch to the nuts. They can be eaten, or not, depending on how spicy you are! Feel free to substitute other nuts for the peanuts, such as cashews or almonds. ☐ A **wok** or stir-fry pan is perfect for this dish because either can take a high heat and give you plenty of room to toss the ingredients fast. If you like, you can use the wok, without washing it, for Any-Day Stir-Fry (page 114) after you make this snack. It will be nicely seasoned and ready to go.

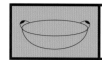

hot woked nuts

1 tablespoon plus 1½ teaspoons light sesame oil

2 jalapeño peppers

1 cup minced scallions (white parts only)

½ teaspoon kosher salt

3 cups (1½ pounds) shelled peanuts

serves 4

Add a little of the oil to the wok or stir-fry pan and, using a paper towel, coat the inside evenly. Slice the jalapeños into circles about ⅛ inch thick and remove most of the seeds.

Heat the wok over medium-high heat until very hot. Add the remaining oil and quickly add the jalapeños, scallions, and salt. Vigorously toss with a big stainless steel spoon for about 1 minute, and then add the peanuts and toss constantly for 2 minutes more, until the nuts are toasted. Transfer to a bowl and serve immediately.

This two-step process yields a fun snack that even kids like! First you make the polenta, and then you cut it into strips and grill them. If the Gorgonzola is a bit too strong for you, a milder cheese, such as fontina, will be just as delicious. I enjoy making the polenta in the classic Italian style, which is a slow procedure. If you are pressed for time, instant polenta is available in most supermarkets. This recipe can easily be doubled. ☐ I recommend using a **double boiler** to make the polenta, which will allow you to cook over very low heat. If you do not have one, you can use a medium saucepan, but you must keep the heat very low or use a diffuser, a metal disk that tempers the flame. You will also need a **grill pan** for this recipe. The ridges in the pan will make very attractive grill marks on the polenta sticks and give them a nice crunchy crust, which insures they stay moist inside. As always, make sure you preheat the grill pan over medium heat until very hot.

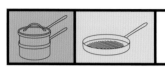

grilled polenta sticks with gorgonzola

4 cups water

1½ teaspoons kosher salt

1 cup medium-grind cornmeal, plus extra for dusting

Extra-virgin olive oil for greasing

½ cup (4 ounces) crumbled Gorgonzola cheese

1 tablespoon chopped fresh flat-leaf parsley

1 teaspoon freshly ground pepper

serves 4

Fill the bottom of a double boiler halfway (about 3 inches) with water and heat to a low simmer. Heat the 4 cups of water in the top of the double boiler to a simmer. Add the salt and then whisk in the polenta slowly. Cook for about 1½ hours, whisking every 15 minutes, or until the polenta is no longer crunchy.

Preheat the oven to 175°F. Line a baking sheet with foil and wipe with oil. Pour the polenta into the pan and allow to cool completely.

Using the foil to help you, turn the cooled polenta out onto a work surface dusted with a little cornmeal. Brush the top with oil and then cut 4-inch strips of polenta about as thick as French fries.

Heat a grill pan over medium heat until very hot. Place the polenta strips, oil side down, in the pan without crowding. Brush the tops with oil. Grill each side for about 2 minutes to brown them, and transfer to a warm platter in the oven. Top with some of the cheese, parsley, and pepper. Keep the polenta sticks in the warm oven while you grill and top the remaining ones.

Grapeseed oil is ideal for this recipe because it can get very hot before it will smoke, but vegetable oil is a good substitute. Buy the highest-quality popcorn kernels for the best flavor. ☐ A large clad stainless steel or anodized aluminum **saucepan** with a tight-fitting lid is the choice for this treat. It does not discolor from the high heat. You will also need hot pads for the lid and handle for the vigorous jiggling necessary to keep the popcorn moving so it cooks evenly and does not stick.

precocious party popcorn balls

SPECIAL EQUIPMENT
clip-on candy thermometer

2 tablespoons grapeseed oil

¹/₃ cup good-quality popcorn
    kernels

1 teaspoon kosher salt

¹/₂ cup light corn syrup

¹/₂ cup molasses

1 teaspoon vinegar

4 tablespoons unsalted butter,
   plus extra for coating your hands

makes 10 to 12 balls

Use a paper towel to wipe the inside of a large saucepan with a little of the oil. Warm the pan over medium heat until hot, about 2 minutes. Add the remaining oil to the pan and increase the heat to medium-high. Add the popcorn kernels, tossing them in the oil to coat well. Cover the pan and shake vigorously while holding the lid down. When the kernels begin to pop, shake the pan constantly until the popping stops, about 3 minutes. Transfer the popcorn to a big bowl and toss well with salt.

Combine the syrup, molasses, and vinegar in the saucepan in which you made the popcorn and stir well. Clip the thermometer onto the side of the pan and bring the mixture to a boil. Continue boiling, stirring occasionally, until the thermometer reads 240°F, then stir constantly until the thermometer reads 270°F. The syrup will instantly harden if you drop a little in cold water. Remove the syrup from the heat and stir in the butter. Pour the syrup over the popcorn and toss to coat quickly. Line a baking sheet with wax paper and rub your hands with butter. Pick up a handful of popcorn and form into 2½- to 3-inch balls. Place the balls on the wax paper. Serve immediately or store in a plastic bag or airtight container.

My friend DK makes the best stuffed eggs I have ever had. We call them "disappearing eggs" because I have never seen any left over. He says to refrigerate eggs for 24 hours after they are boiled to make peeling them easier—he was right!

☐ I tested several methods of boiling eggs for this recipe to discover the perfect amount of water and size of pan needed to cook the eggs evenly. I found that 1 quart of water per egg is the rule—simple as that. If you are making four eggs, you should use a large saucepan. Six eggs need a medium **stockpot,** and so on.

dk's scrumptious stuffed eggs

6 large eggs

6 quarts water

3 tablespoons mayonnaise

1 teaspoon Dijon mustard

½ teaspoon kosher salt

¼ teaspoon freshly ground pepper

2 tablespoons minced fresh flat-leaf parsley

2 teaspoons paprika

makes 12 halves

Put the eggs in a medium stockpot, add the water, and bring to a rapid boil over medium heat. Cover and remove from heat. Let stand for exactly 10 minutes. Using a slotted spoon, transfer the eggs to a bowl of ice water to cool. Peel the eggs immediately or refrigerate them for up to 24 hours, then peel the eggs. Cut them in half lengthwise and remove the yolks, reserving the whites on a platter. In a glass or nonreactive metal bowl, mash the yolks with a fork. Add the mayonnaise, mustard, salt, and pepper and mix well. Stuff the egg halves with the yolk mixture and sprinkle each with a little parsley and paprika. Cover and chill for at least 20 minutes and no more than 3 hours.

variation

Add 3 tablespoons minced bay shrimp to the yolks. Use ¼ teaspoon curry powder instead of the mustard. Garnish with capers instead of parsley and paprika.

Add ¼ cup liver pâté to the yolks. Substitute sour cream for the mayonnaise and omit the mustard. Top with minced cornichon pickles instead of parsley and paprika.

keep it coming tempura

SPECIAL EQUIPMENT
spider strainer and a deep-fat
thermometer

DIPPING SAUCE

1 cup soy sauce

1 teaspoon wasabi powder

One 12-ounce bottle good-quality
  beer

1½ cups cake flour

1½ teaspoons kosher salt

½ teaspoon freshly ground pepper

About 2 quarts peanut oil for
  deep-frying

8 to 12 large shrimp,
  peeled, deveined, tails left on

2 medium sweet potatoes, peeled
  and sliced into ⅛-inch-thick
  rounds

8 ounces trimmed green beans
  (about 1 cup)

1 pound asparagus, cut into
  3-inch pieces (about 1 cup)

8 ounces broccoli florets
  (about 1 cup)

8 ounces carrots, peeled, halved,
  and cut into 3-inch pieces
  (about ½ cup)

You must keep tempura batter cold for the best results. Once it is mixed, put the batter in the refrigerator for 20 minutes while you prepare the vegetables, and refrigerate it while frying each batch too. Allowing the oil to reheat between batches and using cake flour will ensure crispy tempura. Never make all the tempura at once or it will get too soggy. Cook up a batch, serve it immediately, and by the time it has been eaten by family and guests, you can have another batch ready to serve. ☐ A **wok** is ideal for making tempura because it provides plenty of room for even frying. Do not overcrowd the wok. To remove the vegetables and shrimp from the hot oil, you will need a spider strainer—a shallow, round, wire-mesh strainer with a wooden handle, available at most Asian markets. A slotted spoon just does not allow the tempura to drain as well, so a spider is a very good investment.

serves 4 to 6 as an appetizer or 2 to 3 as a main course

To make the dipping sauce: Mix the soy sauce and the wasabi in a small bowl until combined.

In a glass or nonreactive metal bowl, combine the beer, flour, salt, and pepper and stir to blend well. Refrigerate for at least 20 minutes.

Clip the thermometer to a wok and heat about 4 inches of the oil over medium-high heat to 375°F. Dip a couple of shrimp and a few pieces of each vegetable into the batter, coating them completely. Using tongs, carefully add the shrimp and vegetables to the hot oil and fry until golden brown, about 3 minutes. Use the spider strainer to remove everything from the oil and drain on paper towels. Serve immediately with the dipping sauce and repeat the process.

Serve this classic Sicilian dish with good-quality water crackers or crispy bread, or toss it with pasta for a main course. Either way, make the caponata at least 2 hours before you use it. You'll also need a full hour for the eggplant to drain before you can cook it. ☐ This is a perfect dish for a large, deep, straight-sided **sauté pan** so the ingredients have plenty of room to mix and the flavors can marry quickly. A stainless steel or anodized aluminum interior is ideal because it will not react with the vinegar and tomatoes. The burner should be as close to the size of the pan as possible for even heating.

sicilian caponata

serves 4

3½ cups diced unpeeled eggplant (¼-inch dice)

1 tablespoon kosher salt

4 tablespoons olive oil, divided

1 cup finely chopped onion

⅓ cup finely chopped celery

1 cup diced plum tomatoes

⅓ cup chopped pitted green olives

¼ cup red wine vinegar

3 tablespoons chopped capers

3 tablespoons pine nuts, toasted lightly

1 tablespoon sugar

¼ cup finely chopped fresh flat-leaf parsley

Put the eggplant in a colander over a bowl and sprinkle with the salt. Allow it to sit for 1 hour to drain.

Heat 2 tablespoons of the oil in a large sauté pan over medium heat until hot. Shake off as much of the salt from the eggplant as you can and add the eggplant to the oil. Sauté, stirring, for 5 minutes or until tender, and then transfer the eggplant to a bowl or platter and set aside. Add the remaining 2 tablespoons oil to the pan with the onion and cook for about 3 minutes. Then stir in the celery and cook for 5 minutes. Add the tomatoes, olives, vinegar, capers, pine nuts, and sugar and cook the mixture, covered, stirring occasionally, for 5 to 10 minutes, or until it is warmed through and the celery is tender. Remove from the heat. Add the eggplant to the pan, stir in the parsley, and let the mixture cool to room temperature. Cover and chill the caponata for at least 3 hours. When you are ready to serve, allow the caponata to come to room temperature and serve with toasted bread or crackers.

These tempting little packages are a favorite in India. Served from pushcarts on the street, they offer instant gratification to those walking by en route to shopping or strolling with the family. The homemade chutney cools the spicy meat for a

street cart samosas with mango chutney

SPECIAL EQUIPMENT
spider strainer and deep-fat thermometer

MANGO CHUTNEY

1 tablespoon olive oil

1¼ cups finely chopped red onion

¼ teaspoon kosher salt

2 large firm but ripe mangoes, peeled, pitted, and chopped

1 large papaya, peeled, seeded, and chopped

¼ cup distilled white vinegar

¼ cup sugar

1½ teaspoons Chinese five-spice powder

⅛ teaspoon cayenne pepper

2 tablespoons dried currants

SAMOSAS

2 tablespoons olive oil

1½ cups finely chopped sweet onion

¼ teaspoon kosher salt

perfectly balanced combination. If you are pressed for time, you can use a good-quality prepared chutney. ☐ A medium **saucepan** will provide enough room to cook the chutney while keeping it concentrated enough for the flavors to marry. You do not want it too spread out in a larger pan or it will thicken too fast without the flavors developing. A large nonstick **fry pan** is the best choice for making the filling. The low, sloping sides enable you to easily get your big spoon into the pan and separate the meat. A large, wide **soup pot** allows the samosas to cook evenly and the thermometer can clip snugly onto the side so you can stay in tune with the oil temperature, a crucial element for success.

serves 4 to 6

To make the chutney: Heat the oil in a medium saucepan over medium heat. Add the onion and salt. Cover and cook for about 2 minutes, or until soft. Add the mangoes, papaya, vinegar, sugar, five-spice powder, and cayenne pepper. Cook, stirring occasionally, for 10 minutes, or until the mixture starts to thicken. Add the currants and stir well. Remove the saucepan from the heat and allow the chutney to cool to room temperature. Refrigerate for at least 20 minutes and then serve with the freshly made samosas. The chutney can be made 2 to 3 days in advance and stored, covered, in the refrigerator.

To make the samosas: Heat the olive oil in a large nonstick fry pan over medium heat and add the onion and salt. Cover and let cook for about 2 minutes, or until soft. Add the ground beef and, using the back of a spoon, smash it down to break up the big chunks. Once the beef is broken up and starts to brown, add the potato, peas, and curry powder. Stir very well, cover, and cook for 3 minutes, or until the meat is cooked through. Uncover the fry pan and, tilting it to the side, spoon out any excess fat. Stir in the flour. The mixture will thicken slightly. Remove the beef mixture from the heat and set aside, uncovered. Lightly dust a baking sheet with flour and set aside. Arrange a few wonton wrappers on a lightly floured work surface. Spoon about 1 tablespoon of the beef mixture in the center of each wonton wrapper and, using a pastry brush, lightly brush the edges of the wonton wrappers with some of the beaten egg. Fold a corner of the wonton wrapper diagonally over the filling to form a triangle, pinching together the edges. Gently place the filled wonton wrappers on the baking sheet. Repeat the process until all the beef mixture has been used. Refrigerate the wontons, covered with plastic wrap, for at least 20 minutes and up to 8 hours.

With a paper towel, wipe the interior of a large, wide soup pot with a little of the peanut oil. Pour the remaining oil into the pot to a depth of 4 inches and heat over medium-high heat to 375°F. Working in batches, fry the samosas about 2 minutes per side, until they are golden. Using the spider strainer, remove the samosas from the oil and drain on paper towels. Serve immediately with the mango chutney.

1 pound lean ground beef

1 large russet potato, peeled and diced into 1/4-inch cubes

1/4 cup frozen peas, thawed

2 tablespoons curry powder

1 1/2 teaspoons unbleached all-purpose flour, plus extra for dusting

Thirty-six 3-inch wonton wrappers

1 large egg, beaten

About 2 quarts peanut oil for deep-frying

Variations of this dish abound—make it your own. I talked to several accomplished cooks about the concept of the quesadilla, and they all agreed on only two things: Use flour tortillas and watch the heat on the griddle. Some use only one tortilla and fold it over. Others toast one tortilla, cover it with the goodies, place another tortilla on top, and invert the quesadilla to brown the other side; then they cut it like a pizza. You can also try flavored tortillas, which are scented with herbs and spices, for variety. They are available in most major supermarkets. ☐ A **griddle** is one of the handiest pans in a cookware collection. The key to using it properly is preheating it just enough. If the griddle is too hot, the tortilla will burn before the cheese is melted inside. The water test really does work: If you sprinkle a couple of drops of water on a perfectly heated griddle, they will pop, but not smoke. You will need very little oil in this wonderful pan.

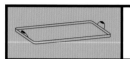

quickest quesadillas

Vegetable oil for greasing

Six 7-inch flour tortillas

3 cups (1 pound) grated cheese such as Cheddar, Monterey jack, or mozzarella, or a blend

1½ cups good-quality salsa

½ cup chopped fresh cilantro, plus whole sprigs for garnish

½ cup sour cream

serves 4

Preheat the oven to 175°F and put an ovenproof platter inside to warm.

Using a paper towel or pastry brush, lightly coat a griddle with a little oil. Heat the griddle over medium heat until hot. Place two of the tortillas on the griddle and sprinkle ½ cup of the cheese over half of each tortilla. Add ¼ cup of the salsa to each one, spreading it evenly over the cheese, and sprinkle with a good pinch of the cilantro. Cook the tortillas for 2 to 3 minutes. They should be light golden brown. Gently fold the tortillas in half and press down with a spatula. Transfer to the warm platter in the oven and repeat with the remaining tortillas, re-oiling the griddle before cooking each quesadilla. Once all the quesadillas are done, cut them in half and garnish with a dollop of sour cream and a sprig of cilantro.

As a home cook, you can make better crab cakes than you will ever find in a restaurant. Classic lump crab cakes are made from blue crabs, which are available year-round but are best from spring through the fall. I have also tried this recipe with Dungeness crab, indigenous to the Pacific Northwest. Be sure that the crab is fresh and do not break up the lumps of meat too much when you form the cakes. I like adding a jalapeño pepper to mine, but you can substitute an equal amount of Anaheim chile if you do not want the heat. Old Bay is a convenient seasoning that is readily available at most supermarkets. Serve the crab cakes as an appetizer or accompany them with a crisp coleslaw for a perfect lunch. ☐ A medium cast-iron **fry pan** is the only choice for these delicate cakes. A golden crispy outside with a moist center is the goal, and the superior heat conductivity of the cast iron makes this effortless. Reheating the pan in between batches is essential, as with all frying.

lumptious crab cakes

1 pound lump crabmeat

½ medium sweet onion, minced

¼ cup good-quality prepared mayonnaise

1 tablespoon minced fresh cilantro

3 tablespoons plain dry breadcrumbs, divided, plus extra as needed

1½ teaspoons Old Bay seasoning

1½ teaspoons minced jalapeño pepper

¼ teaspoon kosher salt

¼ teaspoon ground white pepper

1 large egg, beaten

4 to 5 tablespoons vegetable oil

¼ cup unbleached all-purpose flour

Tartar sauce or cocktail sauce for serving

serves 8 as an appetizer or 4 as a main course

Using your hands, pick through the crabmeat to remove any pieces of shell, but be careful not to break up the lumps too much. With a rubber spatula, gently blend the crabmeat, onion, mayonnaise, cilantro, 2 tablespoons of the breadcrumbs, the Old Bay seasoning, jalapeño, salt, and pepper in a medium bowl. Do not overmix. Fold in the egg. Using your hands, test the mixture to see if it forms a cake. If it is too moist, add more bread crumbs, a little at a time.

Line a baking sheet with wax paper. Using your hands, divide the crab mixture into 4 or 8 even portions and shape into plump, round cakes. Place the cakes on the baking sheet; cover tightly with plastic wrap and chill at least 30 minutes but no more than 24 hours.

continued

Preheat a medium fry pan over medium heat until hot. Add 2 tablespoons of the oil and heat until hot but not smoking. In a shallow bowl, mix the flour and remaining tablespoon of breadcrumbs together. Working in batches, coat the crab cakes in the flour mixture and place in the hot skillet without crowding. Pan fry for 3 minutes or until the bottoms are golden brown and crispy. Using a flat spatula, gently flip the cakes and cook 3 minutes more. Transfer the cakes to a warm platter lined with paper towels. Add the remaining 2 tablespoons oil and cook the rest of the crab cakes. Serve immediately with a good-quality tartar or cocktail sauce.

This dish is very social and a fun appetizer or dinner. If you do serve it as a dinner, a big green salad is really all you need to make a complete meal. The broth should be kept simmering at all times. The meats can be prepared in the morning, refrigerated, and served in the evening. They should be cut into uniform size for a nice presentation and even cooking time. Serve several sauces to dip the meats in for variety. ☐ A **fondue pot** traditionally comes with long forks, but you may also use bamboo skewers that have been soaked in water for 15 minutes. I prefer using a clad stainless steel fondue pot for this recipe and an enameled cast-iron fondue pot for cheese fondue.

mongolian hot pot

8 ounces lean pork, cut into
  ½-inch pieces

8 ounces sirloin steak or filet of
  beef, cut into ½-inch pieces

8 ounces boneless chicken breast
  halves, cut into ½-inch pieces

2 cups watercress

1½ teaspoons olive oil

6 scallions (white and light green
  parts), minced

½ teaspoon kosher salt

6 cups Chicken Stock (page 76)
  or good-quality low-sodium
  canned broth

Assorted dips, such as Chinese
  mustard, soy sauce, plum sauce,
  and barbecue sauce

serves about 10 as an appetizer or 4 to 6 as a main course

Arrange the pork, beef, and chicken on a platter. Provide fondue forks or bamboo skewers. Garnish the platter with watercress. Heat the oil in the fondue pot over medium heat. Add the scallions and the salt. Sauté for about 2 minutes, until the scallions begin to soften. Add the stock and heat to a simmer. Light the alcohol burner that comes with the fondue pot or a sterno can and place it on the bottom of the fondue pan rack. Rest the fondue pot over the flame. Spear a piece of meat and plunge it into the broth. Cook for about 3 minutes, or longer for well-done. When cooked as desired, dip the meat into one of the sauces and eat with a little of the watercress. Repeat with the remaining meat.

Soups and salads are full of goodness, plain and simple. They can begin a meal or be a meal on their own. Here you will find a few basics to build on, such as *Beefy Beef Stock* and *Very Vegetable Soup*, as well as some surprising twists that will become new favorites, like the hearty

Cowboy Chowder and the *Grilled Portobello Mushroom Soup*. Learning how to properly use a heavy soup pot will expand your recipe box of slow-cooked favorites. Soup should never be rushed. A low temperature allows all of the ingredients to cook from the sides as well as from the bottom. Most soups and stews start with a sautéed flavor base before the liquid is added. In this chapter you will also make good use of a fry pan and saucepan for fun salads bursting with flavor and texture, such as *Duck Duck Salad*.

Use a heavy, clad stainless steel **stockpot** or a large enameled cast-iron stockpot for this slow cooking method, which you will use over and over. I love to use my enameled cast-iron pot made by Le Creuset (see Purveyors, page 140) when I make

two stocked stocks

stock as well as other dishes that need to simmer for a while. It is easy to scrape up any bits of the flavor base that stick to the bottom, and the pot retains heat well as the liquid simmers gently on the stove over very low heat.

2 tablespoons vegetable oil, divided

4 pounds beef chuck, cut into 2-inch chunks

2 cups chopped sweet onion

1 cup chopped celery

½ teaspoon kosher salt

¼ teaspoon freshly ground pepper

¾ cup dry red wine

2 pounds small marrow bones

2 quarts boiling water

beefy beef stock

Beef stock should taste like beef, period. To achieve this, use plenty of meat—simple as that. Good-quality cuts of meat, such as chuck, yield fantastic, tender morsels, which you can use for tacos or quesadillas. Please go to the butcher to get your meat and tell him you are making stock. Be sure to ask for small marrow bones, since the marrow is where most of the flavor is.

makes 2 quarts stock

Using a paper towel, wipe the inside of a medium stockpot with a little of the oil. Heat the stockpot over medium heat until hot and add 1 tablespoon of the oil. Brown the beef in batches and transfer it to a platter. Add the remaining oil and then the onion, celery, salt, and pepper. Stir well and reduce the heat to medium-low. Cover the pot and let the onion mixture steam for about 4 minutes, until the onion is soft. Add the wine and simmer, uncovered, for 2 minutes. Add the browned beef and marrow bones to the pot. Cover and cook for 20 minutes without opening the lid to trap the steam. Now, uncover the pot and slowly add the boiling water, being careful not to burn yourself. Stir the

continued

broth very well and return to a boil. Reduce the heat to low and cover with the lid slightly askew. Remove from the heat and allow the stock to simmer, stirring occasionally, for about 2 hours. The meat should be so tender it falls apart. Allow the broth to cool slightly. Position a fine-mesh strainer over a deep bowl and ladle or pour the broth through the strainer. Pick the meat out of the strainer and store in the refrigerator for up to 2 days or freeze for up to 1 month. If using the stock right away, skim off and discard any fat. If not, cool the stock completely, in an ice bath, uncovered. Skim the fat, cover, and refrigerate or freeze. The stock can be kept in the refrigerator for 2 to 3 days or in the freezer for 1 month.

chicken stock

No packaged broths compare with homemade chicken stock. And because it freezes well, I recommend getting those handy resealable containers, portioning out your stock, and storing it in the freezer. Chicken stock is useful for soups, stews, and sauces. Unlike most stock recipes, this one and the beef stock on page 74 require that you develop the flavor base, or *mirepoix*, before adding the other ingredients, resulting in a richer stock. If you prefer, have your butcher chop the chicken for you, but make sure and tell him it is for stock. As with the beef stock, use a large clad stainless steel **stockpot** or enameled cast-iron stockpot.

makes 2 quarts stock

2 tablespoons vegetable oil

2 cups chopped sweet onion

1 cup chopped celery

1 cup chopped carrot

1½ teaspoons kosher salt, divided

4 pounds chicken parts with bones, chopped into pieces

5 quarts boiling water

2 bay leaves

1 tablespoon black peppercorns

Using a paper towel, wipe the inside of a medium stockpot with a little of the oil. Heat the stockpot over medium heat until hot. Add the remaining oil, the onion, celery, and carrot. Sprinkle with ½ teaspoon of the salt, stir well, cover, and cook for about 4 minutes, until the onion is soft. Transfer the onion mixture to a bowl. Allow the stockpot to reheat and, in batches, lightly brown the chicken. When all the chicken is browned, combine the onion mixture and the chicken in the pot. Reduce the heat to low, cover, and cook for about 20 minutes. The chicken should have released some juices. Carefully add the boiling water, bay leaves, peppercorns, and remaining 1 teaspoon salt, and stir well. Bring to a boil, then reduce the heat to medium-low. Cover with the lid slightly askew and simmer for about 1½ hours, stirring occasionally, until the broth is rich and flavorful. Remove from the heat and allow the stock to cool slightly. Pour the stock through a fine- mesh strainer set over a large bowl and discard the solids. If using the stock right away, skim off and discard any fat. If not, cool the stock completely, in an ice bath, uncovered. Skim the fat, cover, and refrigerate or freeze. The stock can be kept in the refrigerator for 2 to 3 days or in the freezer for 1 month.

Many Caribbean countries consider this beans and rice dish a staple. For a tasty and colorful lunch, serve this alongside Smoky Avocado Relish and Crunchy Chips (page 54) and add some Just Right Rice (page 114). You can omit the ham hock if you like, but the dish will not have as full a flavor. The *epazote* is a pungent, wild herb similar to fresh coriander and is available in most Latin markets. ☐ This classic dish

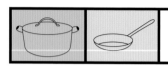

soupy cuban black beans

demonstrates the usefulness of a **Dutch oven.** It is better than a stockpot because it is wide, giving the beans plenty of room to expand. The Dutch oven comes with a tight-fitting lid, which is essential to trap the moisture and flavor of the beans as they slow cook. If you want to serve the beans family style from the pot, make sure to set it on a trivet so the air can circulate all around the pot. Begin by making the flavor base in a nonstick **fry pan** so the ingredients do not stick and they stay moist.

1 pound dried black beans

12 cups water

1 smoked ham hock
(about 8 ounces)

2 medium sweet onions, minced,
divided

12 garlic cloves, minced, divided

1 Anaheim chile, seeded and
diced

3 bay leaves

2½ teaspoons kosher salt, divided

2 tablespoons olive oil

1 small red bell pepper, seeded
and minced

2 teaspoons ground cumin

1 recipe (3 cups) Just Right Rice
for serving (page 114)

Fresh lime juice for serving

¾ cup chopped fresh epazote or
cilantro

Sour cream for serving

serves 6

Carefully pick over the beans, removing any foreign particles, and rinse very well with cold water. In a large Dutch oven or medium stockpot, combine the water, beans, ham hock, half the onions, half the garlic, the chile, bay leaves, and 2 teaspoons of the salt. Bring to a boil over medium-high heat, skimming the surface with a fine-mesh strainer as the froth rises. Reduce the heat to low and simmer, partially covered, for about 2 hours. Stir every 20 minutes for even cooking. If the cooking liquid reduces to the top of the beans, add more warm water. Test several of the beans after about 1¾ hours. They should be tender without splitting open. Remove the pot from the heat, remove the ham hock, and set aside.

Heat a nonstick fry pan over medium heat until hot. Add the oil and then the remaining onions, the bell pepper, the remaining garlic, and the remaining ½ teaspoon salt. Sauté for 8 minutes, or until the vegetables are soft. Add the cumin and sauté for 1 minute more.

To finish the dish, add the mixture in the fry pan to the beans and stir. Spoon ½ cup of rice into each of 6 soup bowls and spoon a generous portion of beans on top. Drizzle a little lime juice over each dish, sprinkle with about 1 teaspoon epazote, and add a dollop of sour cream. Serve immediately.

Nothing else in cookery offers such a creative opportunity as a stew. You can make one from any kind of meat, and the entire spectrum of vegetables, herbs, and sauce combinations awaits your bidding. Most stews, including this one, taste better when made a day in advance, stored in the refrigerator, and then warmed the next day over low heat so the flavors have a chance to marry. Stews always freeze beautifully. Learn how to make a stew properly, and you have found the secret to dozens of different fun dishes. Serve this pot of gold with some crunchy bread and you will have a happy crowd. ☐ This recipe will teach you how to braise meat in a heavy, medium

stockpot or Dutch oven made of clad stainless steel, enameled cast iron, or uncoated cast iron. My favorite is enameled cast iron. It sears the meat well, makes it is easy to scrape up the browned bits of meat from the bottom, and is ideal for simmering.

cowboy chowder

serves 4

Sprinkle the flour over the meat and toss to coat. In a medium stockpot or Dutch oven, heat the fat over medium heat until sizzling. Working in batches, brown the meat on all sides, being careful not to crowd the pot. You do not want too much juice, or the meat will poach instead of brown. As the meat is browned, transfer it to a platter and reserve. Add the onion, celery, carrot, salt, and pepper to the pot. Toss to coat well with the fat and cover. Cook for about 5 minutes, until the onion is soft. Uncover and stir very well, scraping up any browned bits of meat from the bottom of the pan. Add the garlic and cook, stirring frequently, for about 1½ minutes. Add the stock, potatoes, bay leaves, and thyme. Stir well. Bring the mixture to a slow simmer and add the reserved meat. Stir well and cover with the lid slightly askew. Simmer for 45 minutes, or until the meat is tender, stirring occasionally. Serve with crusty bread.

2 pounds boneless beef or a combination of boneless beef, lamb, veal, or pork, cut into 2-inch cubes

½ cup unbleached all-purpose flour

3 tablespoons pork fat or olive oil

1 cup chopped sweet onion

½ cup diced celery

½ cup diced carrot

2 teaspoons kosher salt

1 teaspoon freshly ground pepper

3 cloves garlic, chopped

6 cups Beefy Beef Stock (page 74) or good-quality low-sodium canned beef broth

2 cups diced white rose potato (about 2 medium potatoes)

2 bay leaves

3 sprigs fresh thyme

The sweet portobello mushroom makes for a rich soup that you can also use as a sauce for meat. ☐ Grilling portobello mushrooms in the **grill pan** will fill your kitchen with an enticingly earthy aroma. Properly heating the grill pan is essential for searing in flavor while maintaining moisture. A large **saucepan** is what you need here.

grilled portobello mushroom soup

6 large portobello mushrooms

3 tablespoons extra-virgin olive oil

1 teaspoon kosher salt, divided

½ teaspoon freshly ground pepper, divided

6 cups homemade vegetable stock or good-quality low-sodium canned broth, divided

2 tablespoons unsalted butter

1 medium sweet onion, chopped

2 cloves garlic, minced

½ cup Madeira wine

3 tablespoons unbleached all-purpose flour

1 cup heavy (whipping) cream

1 teaspoon chopped fresh thyme

serves 4 to 6

Clean the mushrooms by gently removing the black gills on the underside with a spoon. Put the mushrooms in a resealable plastic bag and add the oil, ½ teaspoon of the salt, and ¼ teaspoon of the pepper. Seal the bag, shake to coat the mushrooms well, and set aside to marinate for 30 minutes.

Heat a grill pan over medium heat until very hot. Add the mushrooms to the pan and grill for about 15 minutes on each side, or until soft. Let them cool and then chop them into bite-sized pieces. Put half of the mushrooms in a blender or food processor with about 2 cups of the stock and blend until smooth.

Melt the butter in a large saucepan or medium soup pot over medium heat. Add the onions and remaining ½ teaspoon salt. Cover and cook for 3 to 4 minutes, until the onions are soft. Add the garlic and cook for 1 minute more. Add the wine and cook until almost all the liquid has evaporated, about 3 minutes. Stir in the flour and cook for about 2 minutes. Add the remaining 4 cups stock, the mushroom purée, the remaining mushroom pieces, the cream, the remaining ¼ teaspoon pepper, and the thyme. Simmer until thickened, about 15 minutes, and then serve immediately.

Smooth, rich tomato soup and Classic Grilled Cheese (page 44) are a perfect match. I have been dipping the sandwich into the soup since I was a kid. If you haven't tried it, you have been depriving yourself of serious comfort food! ☐ A medium, clad stainless steel **soup pot** is the best choice for this soup because the interior will not react to the acidic tomatoes. The bacon needs to be crisped on medium heat so all the fat is rendered and the bacon is crunchy.

true tomato soup

serves 4

SPECIAL EQUIPMENT
immersion blender

6 slices bacon, chopped into small pieces

2 cups chopped sweet onion

1 teaspoon kosher salt, divided

2 garlic cloves, minced

5 cups chopped ripe tomatoes (about 7 medium tomatoes)

½ cup dry sherry

½ cup dry white wine

4 cups Chicken Stock (page 76) or good-quality low-sodium canned broth

1 tablespoon chopped fresh oregano

1½ teaspoons chopped fresh basil

½ cup heavy whipping cream

¼ teaspoon freshly ground pepper

Heat a medium soup pot over medium heat and add the bacon. Sauté for about 3 minutes, until the bacon starts to crisp. Add the onion and ½ teaspoon of the salt. Cover and cook for about 10 minutes, until the onion is tender and translucent. Add the garlic and sauté for 1 minute more. Add the tomatoes and simmer until they are tender and juicy, stirring occasionally, about 20 minutes. Add the sherry and wine and simmer for 5 minutes more. Add the stock and simmer until the mixture is reduced by about ⅓, about 15 minutes. Stir in the oregano and basil. Let the soup rest off the heat for about 15 minutes to allow the flavors to marry. Use an immersion blender to blend the soup until smooth or, working in batches, purée the soup in a blender and return the soup to the pot. Add the cream and warm over medium heat for about 15 minutes, until heated through but not boiling. Season with the remaining ½ teaspoon salt and the pepper and serve immediately.

The mix of French and Italian influences is what makes this soup so delicious. I learned the trick of putting the cheese rind in the soup from a wonderful friend in Italy. Cut the rind off Parmesan cheese and reserve the cheese for later. Or, better still, get into the habit of saving the rinds in resealable plastic bags in the freezer after you have used up the cheese. □ A wide-bottomed soup pot or Dutch oven is ideal so you can spread the vegetables out and sauté them well.

very vegetable soup

2 tablespoons extra-virgin olive oil

1 cup thinly sliced leeks (white and light green parts), washed thoroughly

1 cup diced sweet onion

1 cup diced carrot

1 cup diced celery

1 teaspoon salt

½ teaspoon freshly ground pepper

8 cups water

One 28-ounce can whole tomatoes, drained and chopped

1½ cups diced russet potato (about 2 medium potatoes)

One 6-by-2-inch Parmesan cheese rind

3 cups baby spinach, stemmed and chopped

¾ cup diced zucchini

¾ cup diced yellow squash

One 15-ounce can cannellini beans, drained and rinsed

1 cup chopped fresh basil

Freshly grated Parmesan cheese for passing

serves 6

Heat the oil in a wide-bottomed soup pot over medium heat. Add the leeks, onion, carrot, celery, salt, and pepper. Stir well to coat the vegetables with the oil. Sauté, stirring occasionally, for about 5 minutes, until the leeks and onion begin to wilt. Add the water, tomatoes, and potatoes. Stir well and add the cheese rind. Bring to a slow simmer and cook for 20 minutes. Add the spinach, zucchini, and squash to the pot and reduce the heat to medium-low. Simmer for about 1 hour, uncovered, stirring occasionally, until all the vegetables are tender. The soup can be made up to this point and refrigerated for 2 to 3 days or frozen for up to 1 month. When you are ready to serve, add the cannellini beans and simmer for 5 to 8 minutes to warm through. Remove the pot from the heat and discard the cheese rind. Ladle the soup into bowls and garnish with basil and cheese.

This salad is based on duck confit, which is made by cooking duck slowly in duck fat. It is a bit of work, but duck confit is so tasty, you will want to use it in other dishes, such as pot stickers or lentils. Plan to start the confit a day or two in advance; the duck must be well salted and then rested in the refrigerator before you cook it. Duck fat can be found at most high-end supermarkets and at gourmet stores, where you will also find the quail eggs. If the fat is frozen, allow it to thaw in the refrigerator. You will be poaching the quail eggs for this salad. If you have never poached an egg before, I recommend you try poaching chicken eggs for practice. ☐ A large, clad stainless steel or enameled cast-iron **saucepan** is best for making the confit because it is deep and wide enough to hold the duck legs and keep them immersed in the fat. Make sure you wipe the interior of the pan very well with the duck fat before cooking. A medium, clad stainless steel saucepan is the perfect size for poaching the eggs so you will be able to get under the eggs gently to remove them without breaking them.

duck duck salad

8 duck legs (about ½ pound each)

5 garlic cloves

3 tablespoons kosher salt

1½ teaspoons freshly ground pepper

6 sprigs fresh thyme

6 cups duck fat

½ cup thinly sliced red onion

½ cup thinly sliced leeks (white and light green parts), washed thoroughly

2 tablespoons balsamic vinegar

8 cups mixed spring greens

About 5 cups water

1 tablespoon distilled white vinegar

8 quail eggs

serves 4 as a main course

In a large resealable plastic freezer bag, combine the duck, garlic, salt, pepper, and thyme. Seal the bag, pressing out the air, and shake very well. Refrigerate for at least 24 hours, and up to 2 days.

Remove the duck from the refrigerator and lift each leg out of the bag, brushing the seasoning off. Reserve on a platter. Using a paper towel, wipe the inside of a large saucepan well with duck fat. Pour the remaining fat into the saucepan and warm over low heat. Just as the duck fat begins to get warm, add the duck legs in a single layer. The duck fat should cover the duck legs completely. Simmer the legs over low to medium-low heat for 3 hours. The

continued

duck fat should have tiny bubbles from the heat—a very mellow simmer. When it is done cooking, the duck meat should fall off the bone very easily.

With tongs, carefully remove the duck legs from the saucepan and drain on a paper towel–lined plate or paper bag. Remove the meat from the bones and reserve. Discard the bones.

Pour the duck fat through a strainer and discard the garlic and thyme. Return 2 tablespoons of the duck fat to the saucepan and heat over medium heat. (Store the remaining duck fat for another use. The duck fat can be strained, refrigerated, and reused for cooking.) Add the onion and leeks and sauté until slightly soft, about 2 minutes. Add the balsamic and remove the pan from the heat.

Rinse and dry the greens in a salad spinner.

Heat the water to a slow boil in a medium saucepan. Add the white vinegar. Poach the quail eggs, 2 at a time to give them plenty of room, for about 1 minute by carefully cracking the eggs into the simmering water. Using a slotted spoon, keep the whites of the eggs from spreading out. Carefully remove the eggs from the water with the slotted spoon and reserve in a dish that is resting close to the saucepan to keep them warm. Repeat with the remaining eggs.

In a large bowl, toss the greens with the leek mixture to coat well. Divide among 4 plates and place generous amounts of duck confit on the greens. Top with 2 eggs per serving. To eat the salad, smash the poached eggs with your fork, allowing the yolk to soak the greens. If you don't use all of the duck, it can be stored in the refrigerator, covered in the fat for several weeks.

Like many one-pot recipes, this recipe can be adapted for any number of meats or shellfish so you can take advantage of whatever looks good in the market. I have used *tasso* (cured pork with Cajun seasonings; see Purveyors, page 140), duck, goose, shrimp, and crawfish, depending on where I am and what is available. Making the roux, a mix of flour and fat used

by you gumbo

to thicken soups and stews, is the first and most important step when cooking gumbo, so take your time. This is not a quick dish, but it will excite your family or guests from the moment they walk in the door and smell the spicy flavors emanating from the kitchen. ☐ This recipe requires a large, heavy pot that will allow you to make the roux slowly so the flour will not burn before it thickens. A **marmite,** also called a bouillabaisse pot, is ideal for this dish, but a large, standard enameled cast-iron soup pot works just as well. You will also need a medium **sauté pan** for browning the meat.

- 1 cup (2 sticks) unsalted butter

- 2 cups unbleached all-purpose flour

- 4 slices bacon

- 3 pounds skinless, boneless chicken breast halves, cut into 2-inch pieces

- 1 pound andouille sausage, sliced ½ inch thick (see Purveyors, page 140)

- 2 medium sweet onions, diced

- 2 teaspoons kosher salt

- 2 celery ribs, diced

- 2 red bell peppers, seeded and diced

- 2 green bell peppers, seeded and diced

- 1 tablespoon chopped garlic

- 5 quarts Chicken Stock (page 76) or good-quality low-sodium canned broth, heated

- 2 teaspoons paprika

- 2 teaspoons dried basil

serves 8 to 10

Melt the butter in a marmite or other large enameled cast-iron pot over medium-low heat. Whisk in the flour until well combined. The mixture will foam a little. Continue cooking, stirring often with a wooden spoon, until the mixture is a dark amber color, about 1 hour.

While the roux is cooking, heat a medium sauté pan over medium heat until hot and add the bacon. Cook until the bacon is crisp and the fat is rendered. Remove the bacon from the pan and drain on paper towels. Save for another use (or even better, snack on it while you're waiting for the gumbo to cook). Add the chicken and sausage to the bacon fat in the pan and sauté until the chicken is just cooked through, about 10 minutes. Remove the pan from the heat and set aside.

Add the onions and salt to the roux and stir well. Add the celery, peppers, and garlic, stirring constantly to mix well. Cook for about 5 minutes, until the onions are soft. Add the hot stock and then the paprika, basil, oregano, thyme, cayenne, pepper, pepper flakes, chili powder, and bay leaves. Once the mixture begins to boil, lower the heat and simmer for 30 minutes. Add the sausage and chicken, stir well, and then add the shrimp. Cook for about 20 minutes more to marry the flavors. Serve in warm bowls over Just Right Rice.

1 teaspoon dried oregano

1 teaspoon dried thyme

1 teaspoon cayenne pepper

1 teaspoon freshly ground pepper

1 teaspoon red pepper flakes

1 teaspoon chili powder

2 bay leaves

16–20 (1 pound) peeled and deveined shrimp

1½ recipes (4½ cups) Just Right Rice (page 114) for serving

Spinach wilts very quickly, so have everything ready, including the plates, when making this dish. Assemble your dining companions when you are ready to toss the spinach with the dressing. I love baby spinach, but it does not hold up well for this salad, so I use the larger, mature leaves. ☐ A large, nonstick **fry pan** is the only one you will need for this salad because you can make the croutons in it first and then use it for the dressing.

just-wilted spinach salad and crunchy croutons

serves 4

4 cups cubed stale baguette

½ cup extra-virgin olive oil, divided

1 teaspoon kosher salt, divided

¼ teaspoon freshly ground pepper

6 to 8 slices best-quality bacon

½ medium red onion, very thinly sliced

8 ounces cremini mushrooms, cleaned and thinly sliced

3 tablespoons balsamic vinegar

12 ounces fresh spinach, stemmed, washed very well, and dried in a salad spinner

4 hard-boiled eggs, chopped

Toss the bread cubes with half of the oil and season with ½ teaspoon of the salt and the pepper. Heat a large nonstick fry pan over medium heat until very hot. Add the remaining oil to the pan. Add the bread cubes and fry, turning several times, until golden and crisp on all sides, about 5 minutes. Transfer the croutons to a paper towel–lined plate.

Add the bacon to the pan and cook until crispy on both sides, about 10 minutes. Transfer the bacon to a paper towel–lined plate to drain and cool slightly. Then roughly chop to make bite-sized pieces.

Discard all but about 3 tablespoons of oil from the pan. Add the onion and the remaining ½ teaspoon salt. Sauté for about 3 minutes, until soft. Add the mushrooms and vinegar and continue cooking for 3 minutes more. Remove the pan from the heat and return the bacon to the pan.

Put the spinach in a large salad bowl. When you are ready to serve, drizzle the warm bacon dressing over the spinach and toss quickly. Divide the spinach mixture evenly among 4 salad plates, sprinkle some of the egg on top of each, and then add croutons. Serve immediately.

Dinnertime is such a grand opportunity to show off—so why not? That does not mean that it has to be difficult. Be bold and try these recipes while expanding your cookware assortment. Several dishes here will teach you timing as you work with more than one piece of cookware, such as

main dishes and sidekicks

New Zealand Leg of Lamb with Lavender-Laced Lilies au Gratin and *Blackened Rib Eyes with Saucepan Potatoes*. Take your time and refer to the methods section (page 21) if you are not sure about how to do something. Prepping the side dish in advance is always helpful, and look to each recipe to tell you when to start cooking the side dishes.

Southern memories of this dish from childhood make me weak in the knees. The aroma is so intoxicating it will be difficult to keep the family out of the kitchen. The dumplings must be served immediately, so call everyone to the table right before

chicken and dumplings

you finish them. Please use the best-quality chicken you can find, preferably a kosher one, for the cleanest, tastiest broth. I prefer to use Bisquick for the dumplings, but you can also use a recipe for baking powder biscuits. ☐ Like all slow-cooking soups and stews, this needs a heavy pot to retain the heat. A large enameled cast-iron **soup pot** or Dutch oven is best. You can brown the chicken first and then add all the other ingredients to the same pot.

1 cup unbleached all-purpose flour

1/2 teaspoon kosher salt

1/4 teaspoon freshly ground pepper

4 pounds chicken parts, washed and patted dry

2 tablespoons unsalted butter

1 tablespoon vegetable oil

6 leeks (white and light green parts), thinly sliced crosswise and washed thoroughly (about 2 cups)

6 shallots, minced

6 medium carrots, peeled and diced

2 celery ribs with leaves, diced

2 bay leaves

1/2 teaspoon dried thyme, crumbled

4 cups Chicken Stock (page 76) or good-quality low-sodium canned broth

1/2 cup apple cider or juice

serves 4

Stir together the flour, salt, and pepper in a pie pan or on a plate. Dredge the chicken parts in the flour, shaking off the excess, and put them on a wire baking rack.

Melt the butter in a soup pot over medium heat. Add the oil, and when it is warm, use tongs to add 4 or 5 pieces of the chicken, being careful not to crowd them. Brown for about 10 minutes on each side, until they begin to crisp and are light brown. Transfer the chicken to a plate as it is finished and repeat until all the chicken is cooked.

Add the leeks and shallots to the soup pot. Use a spoon to scrape up the brown bits on the bottom of the pot and cook the leeks and shallots for 3 to 4 minutes, until wilted. Add the carrots, celery, bay leaves, and thyme. Stir well and cook the vegetables for 3 minutes. Stir in the stock and cider, deglazing the pan. Bring to a boil and add the chicken pieces. Reduce the heat and simmer, with the lid slightly askew, for about 30 minutes, until the chicken begins to separate from the bone.

To make the dumplings: While the chicken is cooking, in a glass or nonreactive metal bowl, combine the Bisquick, milk, egg, and salt. Mix with a fork until barely moist. Drop by spoonfuls into the chicken stock and cover. Cook for 12 minutes, or until the dumplings float. The dumplings should look like little clouds floating in the stock. Using a slotted spoon, transfer the dumplings into bowls. Ladle the broth, chicken, and vegetables over the dumplings and serve immediately.

DUMPLINGS
1 cup Bisquick

$1/2$ cup milk

1 large egg, beaten well

$1/4$ teaspoon kosher salt

new zealand leg of lamb with lavender-laced lilies au gratin

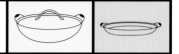

The simple technique of braising is what transforms this lamb into sweet, succulent, tender meat dripping with flavor. Accompanied by a colorful assortment of onions, the lamb looks and tastes like it was made in a four-star kitchen. Lamb is the only meat besides beef that is best served rare. An instant-read thermometer will indicate when it is done to perfection. Allowing the meat to rest is key to insuring success. If you have any leftovers, a favorite meal of mine is cold lamb sandwiches with spicy mustard. The Lilies au Gratin is a beautiful dish that can vary with the assortment of available onions, which are, in fact, related to the lily family. I prefer finding the smallest, sweetest, and most colorful. The produce company Melissa's (see Purveyors, page 140) has a wonderful variety. Lavender is a member of the mint family and can be found in specialty gourmet markets (see Purveyors, page 140). ☐ A stainless steel **braiser pan** is ideal for the lamb. It is one of my favorites because searing the meat in this pan produces great bits of flavor, which get incorporated into the dish. Do not be afraid to use a heavy stainless steel utensil to release the meat and scrape up the bits. For the "lilies," you will need a **gratin pan**, another one of my favorites. It allows you to sauté, bake in the oven, and then serve at the table from the same pan. Cast-iron, porcelain, or tempered glass are all great materials for the gratin dish.

serves 6 to 8

continued

SPECIAL EQUIPMENT
instant-read thermometer

LEG OF LAMB

One 6- to 7-pound leg of lamb

8 garlic cloves

1 teaspoon kosher salt

1 teaspoon freshly ground pepper

1½ tablespoons olive oil

½ cup light and fruity red wine, such as Beaujolais

LILIES AU GRATIN

2 tablespoons unsalted butter

8 ounces baby red onions, peeled

8 ounces baby Vidalia onions, peeled

8 ounces small shallots, peeled

4 garlic cloves, peeled and sliced

½ teaspoon kosher salt

¼ teaspoon freshly ground white pepper

½ cup heavy whipping cream

1 tablespoon dried lavender

½ cup pecorino or Parmesan cheese

Preheat the oven to 400°F.

To prepare the leg of lamb: With a sharp knife, make ¼-inch slits in the flesh and insert the garlic cloves. Season with the salt and pepper. With a paper towel, wipe the inside of a braiser pan with a little of the oil. Preheat the pan over medium heat and add the remaining oil. Place the leg of lamb, fat side down, in the pan. Cook until it begins to crisp, about 10 minutes. Turn over the lamb and cook for 5 minutes more to brown the other side. Slowly add the wine and deglaze the pan, scraping up the browned bits. Carefully place the pan in the oven and braise the lamb about 1½ hours, or until an instant-read thermometer registers 140°F when placed into the thickest part of the meat for rare; 150°F for medium.

Meanwhile, to make the Lilies au Gratin: In a gratin pan, melt the butter over medium-low heat and immediately add the onions, shallots, and garlic to the pan. Add the salt and pepper and toss the mixture well. Sauté until the onions just begin to brown, about 10 minutes. Add the cream slowly, and then the lavender. Bring to a slow simmer, gently stirring constantly. Cook for 15 minutes, or until the mixture begins to thicken. When the lamb has about 20 minutes of roasting time left, sprinkle the cheese on top of the onion mixture and place the "lilies" in the oven for 20 minutes. They should develop a crispy, golden crust and be hot and bubbly.

Remove the lamb from the oven and turn off the oven, leaving the Lilies au Gratin inside. Transfer the lamb to a serving platter, and allow it to rest with a foil tent over it for 15 to 20 minutes before carving. After carving the lamb, remove the Lilies au Gratin from the oven and serve immediately with the lamb.

Scallops are little jewels from the sea that are quick and easy to cook. Trust a New Englander when looking for the best in your area. Cape Bay and "diver" scallops are the first choice; they should be ivory colored and about an inch or so in diameter. ☐ Sufferin' Succotash is a colorful dish that is a summer favorite and a wonderful addition to many main courses, such

seashore seared scallops and sufferin' succotash

as 'Tucky Fried Chicken (page 109). It should be made first and set aside while you make the scallops in the same pan. Toss the ingredients by using the classic pan-flipping method of jerking the pan forward and then back quickly. Most utensils are likely to break up the vegetables, so toss carefully. For a visually appealing dish, the vegetables should all be about the same size. ☐ The scallops will introduce you to the technique of searing. The key to soft, tender scallops is only turning them once and not overcooking them. Searing is always quick, and I have found that a medium, clad stainless steel or anodized aluminum **fry pan** achieves a golden-colored scallop that is crispy on the outside and soft and tender inside. A cast-iron pan will not work here because it will react to the acidic wine.

serves 4

To make the succotash: Heat a medium fry pan over medium heat until hot. Add the oil and then the onion. Toss to coat the onion with the oil and sprinkle with ¼ teaspoon of the salt. Cover the pan and steam the onion for 2 minutes, until soft. Add the peppers and then the garlic. Toss the ingredients very well, and sauté for 2 more minutes. Add the asparagus tips, toss well again, then add the corn and beans. Add the remaining ½ teaspoon of salt and the pepper and

continued

SUCCOTASH

2 tablespoons olive oil

1 medium red onion, diced

¾ teaspoon kosher salt, divided

1 red bell pepper, seeded and diced

1 yellow bell pepper, seeded and diced

2 garlic cloves, minced

1 pound asparagus, tips sliced on the bias about 2 inches from the top

2 cups fresh corn kernels

2 cups cooked lima beans

¼ teaspoon freshly ground pepper

SCALLOPS

1 pound 8 ounces sea scallops

¾ teaspoon kosher salt, divided

½ teaspoon freshly ground pepper, divided

continued

toss very well again. Sauté for 2 to 3 minutes, tossing all the while, or until the asparagus is bright green and still slightly crunchy. Serve immediately or transfer to a warm serving bowl and cover while you make the scallops.

To make the scallops: Using the tip of a knife, remove the small protruding tendon from each scallop. Sprinkle the scallops on both sides with ½ teaspoon of the salt and ¼ teaspoon of the pepper. Heat a medium fry pan over medium heat until hot and add 1 tablespoon of the butter. Swirl the butter as it melts and begins to cook, until it is light golden in color. Working quickly, add half of the scallops, one at a time, flat sides down. Sear for about 2 minutes, until they begin to brown around the edges. Using tongs, carefully turn the scallops, one at a time, and cook for 1 minute more, until barely cooked through. Transfer the scallops to a warm platter and cover with foil. Add another 1 tablespoon butter to the pan and sear the remaining scallops. Transfer the scallops to the platter, add the shallots to the pan, and cook for 2 minutes, or until soft. Add the wine and simmer for 6 or 7 minutes, until reduced by one-third. Add the zest and stir well. Remove the pan from the heat, stir in the remaining 2 tablespoons butter, the parsley, lemon juice, and the remaining ¼ teaspoon salt and ¼ teaspoon pepper. Spoon the sauce over the scallops and serve immediately with the Sufferin' Succotash.

4 tablespoons unsalted butter, divided

1 medium shallot, minced

1 cup dry white wine

1½ teaspoons grated lemon zest

2½ tablespoons minced fresh flat-leaf parsley

1 tablespoon fresh lemon juice

blackened rib eyes with saucepan potatoes

SAUCEPAN POTATOES

6 to 8 Yukon gold potatoes, peeled (about 2½ pounds)

1½ teaspoons kosher salt

3 tablespoons half-and-half

1 tablespoon unsalted butter

½ teaspoon freshly ground pepper

1 tablespoon paprika

2 teaspoons salt

1 teaspoon freshly ground pepper

1 teaspoon garlic powder

1 teaspoon cayenne pepper

½ teaspoon dried oregano

½ teaspoon dried thyme

3 tablespoons unsalted butter, melted

Four 10-ounce rib-eye steaks, at room temperature

These steaks are dredged in a savory seasoning and seared in a dry red-hot pan, which is what blackening is all about. ☐ Only a medium to large cast-iron **fry pan** will do when you blacken because it conducts the heat so well. I have a cast-iron fry pan that I only use for blackening. A piping hot pan seals the flavor in the meat quickly, and the inside stays moist and tender. Use a medium **saucepan** to cook the potatoes.

serves 4

Preheat a large cast-iron skillet over medium heat until very hot, 20 minutes.

Meanwhile, to make the potatoes: Put them in a medium saucepan and add enough water to cover them. Add the salt and bring to a slow boil over medium heat. Set the cover askew and cook until the potatoes can easily be pierced with a sharp knife, about 20 minutes. Do not boil too hard or the potatoes will fall apart. Remove from the heat and drain, reserving about ¼ cup water in the pan.

In a small bowl, combine the paprika, salt, pepper, garlic powder, cayenne, oregano, and thyme. Transfer to a plate or pie pan. Brush the steaks with the butter and dredge in the spice blend. Turn the heat up to medium-high for 1 minute and place the steaks in the pan without crowding. It will smoke and be very hot. Sear or blacken the steaks for about 3 minutes and then turn and finish to desired doneness, about 3 minutes more for medium-rare, 4 minutes more for medium.

Using a potato masher, beat the potatoes while adding the half-and-half, butter, and pepper. Continue beating until smooth. Serve immediately.

lobster thermidor and garlic broccoli

Lobster is already considered a luxury by most, and this classic dish takes it to the ultimate level in decadence. Freshly cooked lobster meat is combined with rich, creamy sauce and then stuffed into the lobster shells, which are sprinkled with bread crumbs and broiled. If you do not want to use whole lobsters, frozen tails will work as well but will not make as dramatic a presentation. You can also substitute lemon juice for the sherry if you wish.

☐ A large **steamer insert** in a large **saucepan** is my choice for cooking the lobsters. It is much better than immersing them in water and boiling them. The meat stays firm, yet tender. Or you can use a fish poacher with 1 inch of boiling water. To make the sauce, I like to use a medium **fry pan**. It can be nonstick, but I prefer a clad stainless steel pan so I don't have to worry about scratching the coating when I use the whisk. ☐ The bright green broccoli is an attractive side for numerous dishes, but is especially beautiful paired with the lobster. It is very easy to make, but be sure not to overcook it. This method is a combination of simmering and sautéing, so the florets stay crisp and tender. Use a medium **sauté pan** with a lid for this dish to give the broccoli plenty of room to cook evenly.

serves 4

Prepare your steamer by adding water to a large saucepan and heat the water over medium heat—not high—until the water is simmering steadily but not boiling rapidly. Put the lobsters in the steamer, set over the saucepan, one or two at a time, depending on how big your steamer is. Do not crowd the

continued

Ingredients

4 live 1½-pound Maine lobsters

4 tablespoons unsalted butter, plus 2 tablespoons melted

4 ounces cremini mushrooms, sliced

1 teaspoon minced fresh tarragon

1 teaspoon sherry

3 tablespoons unbleached all-purpose flour

2 cups half-and-half

2 teaspoons mustard powder

½ teaspoon kosher salt

¼ teaspoon freshly ground pepper

1 large egg yolk

1 cup fine plain dry bread crumbs

GARLIC BROCCOLI

2½ cups (about 1½ pounds) broccoli florets

½ teaspoon kosher salt

1 tablespoon extra-virgin olive oil

4 garlic cloves, peeled and sliced

1 tablespoon fresh lemon juice

¼ teaspoon freshly ground pepper

lobsters. Steam for 15 minutes, or until they turn bright red. Using tongs, remove the lobsters from the steamer and lay them on their backs to cool. Once they are cool enough to handle, crack the shells, remove the meat. Cut it into bite-sized pieces. Rinse the shells well for restuffing. Set aside the shells and meat.

Melt the 4 tablespoons butter in a medium fry pan over medium heat. Add the mushrooms and tarragon and sauté gently until the mushrooms are soft, about 5 minutes. Using a slotted spoon, transfer the mushrooms to a glass or nonreactive metal bowl, sprinkle with the sherry, and set aside. Whisk the flour into the butter in the fry pan. Allow it to cook until it bubbles, about 2 minutes, but do not let it brown. Add a little of the half-and-half at a time, whisking constantly until creamy and smooth after each addition. Once all of the half-and-half has been added, stir in the mustard, salt, and pepper, and then whisk in the egg yolk. Remove the pan from the heat and allow the mixture to cool slightly. Fold in the lobster meat and reserved mushrooms, blending well. Stuff the lobster shells with the mixture. Mix the melted butter with the bread crumbs and sprinkle the mixture on top of the lobster. You can make this dish up to this point and keep the lobsters in the refrigerator, covered, for up to 6 hours.

When you are ready to serve, preheat the broiler. Line a broiling pan or oven-proof baking dish with foil and place the lobsters under the broiler to heat the lobsters and crisp the breadcrumbs, 12 to 15 minutes.

Meanwhile, to make the broccoli: Heat about 2 inches of water to a simmer in a medium sauté pan over medium heat. Add the broccoli and salt. Cover and cook for 2 minutes. Uncover and allow the water to completely evaporate, about 2 minutes. The broccoli should be cooked perfectly by the time the water is gone. Drizzle the oil over the broccoli and add the garlic. Sauté the broccoli and garlic for about 1 1/2 minutes, tossing all the while. The garlic should be just fragrant but not crispy. Drizzle the lemon juice on the broccoli and then season with pepper and additional salt if you like. Transfer the lobsters to warm plates and serve immediately with the Garlic Broccoli.

pretty poached salmon and charming couscous

2½ cups dry white wine, divided

1 tablespoon peppercorns

Grated zest of 1 lemon

One 2-inch piece fresh peeled ginger

Four 6-ounce salmon fillets, picked over for small bones

CHARMING COUSCOUS

4 cups low-sodium vegetable broth

2 tablespoons unsalted butter

1 teaspoon kosher salt

Two 10-ounce boxes quick-cooking couscous (3½ cups)

2 tablespoons chopped fresh flat-leaf parsley

3 plum tomatoes, chopped

1 heaping tablespoon drained capers, coarsely chopped

4 tablespoons cold unsalted butter, cut into small pieces

1 teaspoon chopped fresh flat-leaf parsley

½ teaspoon kosher salt

¼ teaspoon freshly ground pepper

Poaching is an enjoyable and easy way to make the most popular fish in America. You can also try this method with halibut, grouper, and bass. The poaching liquid is the most important part of this dish, and the most fun to experiment with. The crucial rule is that it should be highly seasoned to give the fish flavor. For weight watchers, this method is worth knowing because no oil is used. ☐ A **fish poacher** is convenient because of the handy insert that assists in removing the cooked fish. It is very important that you fill the poacher with only 2 inches of water, as instructed, because it becomes the base for the sauce. Several small fillets can be cooked at once. To make the sauce you will need a medium **saucier.** The curved sides allow a whisk to easily blend the sauce. ☐ Couscous, a light North African dish, is made from granules of semolina, which is actually pasta. Unlike pasta, however, it is not boiled. Once you add the dry couscous to the boiling hot water you must turn the heat off and let it rest. A large **saucepan** with a lid is all you will need for this dish.

serves 4

Pour water into a fish poacher to a depth of 2 inches. Add 2 cups of the wine, the peppercorns, zest, and ginger. Heat the liquid to a gentle simmer over medium heat. Reduce the heat to medium-low. Rinse and dry the fillets. Place them, skin sides down, on the poaching rack and lower it into the liquid. Cover the pan and poach the salmon for 10 minutes, or until a knife gently inserted goes through the fillets easily.

continued

Meanwhile, to make the couscous: Bring the broth to a boil with the butter and salt in a large saucepan. Stir in the couscous, cover, and remove from the heat. Let stand 5 minutes, then fluff with a fork. Gently fold in the parsley and tomatoes. Replace the cover and set aside until ready to serve.

Transfer the fillets to a warm platter and cover with foil. Pass the poaching liquid through a strainer, reserve ¼ cup for the sauce, and discard the rest.

To make the sauce: In a medium saucier, heat the remaining ½ cup wine over medium heat and reduce it to ¼ cup, about 4 minutes. Add the reserved poaching liquid and simmer for about 4 more minutes, until the liquid is reduced to about ⅓ cup. Add the capers and whisk in the butter, a little at a time, to incorporate it into the sauce. Remove the sauce from the heat and whisk in the parsley, salt, and pepper. Spoon the sauce over the salmon fillets and serve immediately with the couscous.

'tucky fried chicken and gracious gratin

There are three regional styles of fried chicken that I know of: Southern, Northwestern, and Northeastern. The first cooking step is where the crucial difference lies. The chicken pieces are dipped in cream in the Northwest, in egg in the Northeast, and in the South—my favorite version—soaked in buttermilk and then dredged in flour. It may seem old-fashioned, but the best thing to use for perfectly fried chicken is still good ol' vegetable shortening. In the South, one of the truly indigenous cultures of America, we drain our chicken as it comes out of the piping hot oil on paper grocery bags lined with a single layer of paper towel on top—it works. ☐ A well-seasoned cast-iron **sauté pan** is the only pan that will produce authentic Southern fried chicken. No other material holds the heat well enough to get a crispy exterior. ☐ Everyone likes au gratin potatoes—piping-hot and cheesy! ☐ The shallow **gratin pan** is perfectly designed to allow everyone to get a piece of the action—that crunchy, yummy top! The pan is available in many different materials, which are all suitable, including clad stainless steel, enameled cast iron, porcelain, and glass.

serves 4

Preheat the oven to 350°F. In a glass or nonreactive metal bowl, soak the chicken in the buttermilk, refrigerated, for 1 hour.

Meanwhile, to make the gratin: Wipe the inside of a gratin pan with some of the butter and melt the remaining butter in the pan over low heat. Once it starts to bubble, add the leeks, 1 teaspoon of the salt, and the white pepper. Sauté the

continued

One 2½-pound broiler chicken, cut into pieces, washed, and patted dry

1 cup buttermilk

GRACIOUS GRATIN

2½ tablespoons unsalted butter

3 leeks (white and light green parts), thinly sliced crosswise and washed thoroughly

3 teaspoons kosher salt, divided

¼ teaspoon freshly ground white pepper

2 garlic cloves, minced

3 pounds russet potatoes, peeled and thinly sliced

2 cups heavy whipping cream

½ cup whole milk

3 ounces fontina cheese, grated

1½ teaspoons paprika

¾ cup unbleached all-purpose flour

½ teaspoon freshly ground pepper

½ cup vegetable shortening

leeks until soft, about 3 minutes. Add the garlic and sauté for 1 minute more. In a medium glass or nonreactive metal bowl, toss the potatoes with the cooked leeks. Combine the cream and milk in a pitcher or bowl. Return half of the potatoes to the gratin pan and add half of the cream mixture. Sprinkle half of the cheese on top. Add the remaining potatoes to the gratin pan, arranging them so the slices lie flat or in a pinwheel design. Cover the potatoes with the remaining cream and cheese. Sprinkle the paprika on top. The dish can be made up to this point, covered, and refrigerated for up to 1 day or frozen for up to 1 month, thawed in the refrigerator, and then baked. Cover the pan with foil and bake for 45 minutes. Remove the foil and bake for 20 minutes more, or until the top is golden brown. Remove the potatoes and allow them to rest for 10 to 15 minutes before serving.

While the gratin is baking, combine the flour, remaining 2 teaspoons salt, and black pepper in a paper bag. Drain the chicken and place each piece, one at a time, in the bag and shake so that the chicken is completely covered with the flour.

Heat the shortening in a large cast-iron sauté pan over medium heat until very hot and sizzling. It should be about $\frac{1}{2}$ inch deep. Using tongs, carefully place a few chicken pieces into the skillet, skin sides down, being careful not to over-crowd the pan. Fry until browned and crispy, about 10 minutes on the first side and 5 minutes on the second side. Drain each piece on a paper towel or paper bag and then place on an ovenproof platter. Reheat the shortening and fry the remaining chicken. Once all the chicken is fried, put the platter in the oven to crisp for 20 minutes, then serve with the gratin.

Steak Diane, with its creamy peppercorn sauce, is a favorite of mine, and inspired this dish. Almost everyone likes grilled steak, but hold onto your hat when you taste a pan-seared steak with a luscious sauce suitable for finger licking or sopping up with a crusty baguette. Serve this dish with Saucepan Potatoes (page 102) or Just Right Rice (page 114). You can mix your own pepper blend, but it's easier to purchase a blend that includes Tellicherry, white, and green peppercorns and put it in your grinder. ☐ A large, clad stainless steel **fry pan** is my preference, although anodized aluminum would also work

sassy sauced steak and green beans with almonds

here. The steaks will brown quickly, you will then be able to scrape up the browned bits that enhance the sauce, and the pan will not react with the brandy. ☐ I like serving the green beans dish as a side very often in the summer, when I can get fresh Kentucky green beans. It is one of those simple recipes that you can make whenever you see these crisp, fresh beans in the market. Take care to trim them well. Most just need a little nip of the knife on both ends to prepare them for cooking. A medium **saucepan** with a tight-fitting lid allows you to toss the beans with the melted butter to coat them evenly. This is a trick I also use to make carrots.

serves 4

1½ **pounds fresh Kentucky green beans (about 3 cups)**

2 **teaspoons kosher salt**

1 **tablespoon unsalted butter or extra virgin olive oil**

¼ **cup slivered almonds**

SASSY SAUCED STEAK

2 to 3 **tablespoons freshly ground mixed peppercorns**

1½ **teaspoons kosher salt**

Four 8-ounce **New York strip steaks (½ inch thick)**

2 **tablespoons unsalted butter**

¼ **cup brandy**

½ **cup heavy whipping cream**

2 **tablespoons chopped fresh flat-leaf parsley**

Trim the beans, put them in a medium saucepan, and cover with water. Add the salt and heat to a mellow simmer over medium heat until just tender, about 15 minutes. Do not overcook; the green beans should still be crisp. Drain off the water.

continued

Meanwhile, to make the steaks: Mix the pepper and salt in a shallow dish and coat the steaks very well with the mixture. Melt the butter over medium heat in a large fry pan until hot but not browned. Add the steaks and sear for 4 minutes on the first side, then turn and brown for 3 minutes more for medium-rare or until desired doneness. Transfer the steaks to a warm platter to rest.

Add the brandy to the pan and deglaze by scraping up any browned bits on the bottom of the pan. Allow the brandy to simmer for 1 minute. Slowly whisk in the cream and continue whisking until the sauce is blended. Return the steaks and any juice on the platter to the pan and remove the pan from the heat.

To finish the beans: Add the butter and almonds to the pan and return the pan to medium heat to melt the butter. Remove the pan from the heat, place the lid on the pan, and with one hand on the lid and the other holding the handle, shake the pan vigorously to coat the beans.

To serve, transfer the steaks to warm plates with tongs and spoon the sauce on top. Garnish with the parsley and accompany with the green beans.

The fish can be stuffed and refrigerated ahead of time, freeing you up to relax before dinner. The carrots get their name—and flavor—from dried tarragon. ☐ A large nonstick **sauté pan** will help you to gently crisp the exterior of the sole without the fish falling apart. It should be hot, but not smoking. A **saucepan** is perfect for the carrots.

crab-stuffed dover sole and tarry carrots

serves 4

Season the fillets on both sides with the salt and pepper. In a medium glass or nonreactive metal bowl, combine the crabmeat, breadcrumbs, egg, and parsley. Mix well. Using your hands, spread a layer of the crab mixture on 1 side of each fillet and roll up from one end to the other.

To make the carrots: Put the carrots in a medium saucepan. Add the salt and barely cover the carrots with water. Heat to a boil over a medium flame and cook until the carrots are tender when tested with a knife, about 10 minutes.

Meanwhile, heat the oil in a large nonstick sauté pan over medium heat until hot. Add the rolled fillets to the pan and cook for 3 to 4 minutes, until golden and crispy on the bottom. Gently roll the fillets over and cook the other side until golden, another 3 minutes. Transfer the fillets to a platter and set aside. Add the wine to the pan to deglaze it and simmer until reduced by half, about 3 minutes. Stir in the cream and capers and simmer for 3 minutes more. Return the fillets to the pan, remove from the heat, and cover to keep warm.

Drain any remaining water from the carrot pan and add the butter and tarragon. Cover and shake vigorously to coat the carrots well. Serve immediately.

Four 7-ounce Dover sole fillets

$\frac{1}{2}$ teaspoon kosher salt

$\frac{1}{4}$ teaspoon freshly ground pepper

1 cup (8 ounces) lump crabmeat

$\frac{1}{4}$ cup coarse breadcrumbs

1 large egg, beaten

1 tablespoon chopped fresh flat-leaf parsley

1 tablespoon olive oil

$\frac{1}{2}$ cup dry white wine

$\frac{1}{4}$ cup heavy whipping cream

1 tablespoon capers, drained

TARRY CARROTS

2 cups peeled and sliced carrots or about 20 baby carrots, peeled

$\frac{1}{2}$ teaspoon kosher salt

1 tablespoon unsalted butter

1 tablespoon dried tarragon

any-day stir-fry and just right rice

Marinate some beef, chicken, or pork, toss it with some colorful vegetables, accompany the masterpiece with jasmine rice, and voilà—you have a great easy meal in minutes. ☐ This recipe is ideal for learning how to use a **wok** or stir-fry pan. To stir-fry, get the pan piping hot and stir and flip the ingredients for a short cooking time. ☐ Perfect rice is not difficult, honest. I like the jiggle method: Once or twice during cooking, hold down the lid and jiggle the pot to make sure the rice cooks evenly. Stirring rice is never a good idea because the rice will become gummy. The jiggling keeps it from sticking and ensures fluffy "just right" rice. It can be made, cooled to room temperature, and refrigerated in a closed container for up to 1 week. To reheat, spoon the rice into a microwave-safe container and sprinkle a little water on top. Microwave on high heat for about 1½ minutes. A medium **saucepan** with a tight-fitting lid is all you need.

¼ cup soy sauce

5 garlic cloves, minced

2 tablespoons honey

1 tablespoon dark sesame oil

½ jalapeño pepper, seeded and minced

8 ounces boneless beef, chicken, or pork, cut into 2-inch strips

JUST RIGHT RICE
makes 3 cups

1 cup jasmine or basmati rice

2 cups water

1 teaspoon kosher salt

2 tablespoons light sesame oil or olive oil

1 tablespoon cornstarch

½ cup (4 ounces) cashews, toasted

6 ounces scallions (white and light green parts), sliced on the diagonal

1 red bell pepper, seeded and cut into ¼-inch strips

1 yellow bell pepper, seeded and cut into ¼-inch strips

2 celery ribs, sliced on the diagonal

serves 4

Combine the soy sauce, 3 cloves of the minced garlic, the honey, sesame oil, and jalapeño in a medium glass or nonreactive metal bowl. Add the meat and toss to coat well. Cover and refrigerate for at least 1 hour and no more than 12 hours.

Meanwhile, to make the rice: Rinse the rice under cool water to remove some of the starch. Combine the water, rice, and salt in a medium saucepan. Cover and bring to a slow simmer over medium-low heat. Holding the top down, jiggle the pan a little to stir up the rice. Continue cooking for 20 minutes, and then remove from the heat and jiggle the pan again. Crack the lid to let some of the heat out. Leave the lid cracked and allow the rice to rest for 5 minutes. Fluff with a fork and serve immediately or cool completely, cover, and refrigerate.

Wipe the interior of a wok or stir-fry pan with a little oil and heat over medium heat until hot. Sprinkle the cornstarch over the meat to coat well. Add 1 tablespoon of the oil to the pan and then the cashews. Toss well. Add the meat and stir-fry, stirring constantly, for 2 minutes, until browned. Transfer the meat and cashews to a dish and set aside. Add the remaining tablespoon of oil and then the scallions and peppers. Stir-fry for about 1½ minutes, stirring constantly. Add the celery, toss well, and then add the remaining 2 cloves garlic. Return the meat to the pan and cook, tossing well, for 1½ minutes more until piping hot. Serve immediately over the Just Right Rice.

This famous French seafood stew can vary, depending on where you live. Use whatever fish and shellfish are in season in your area to create your own signature style. The key is to develop the flavor base or mirepoix and then lower the heat so the shellfish cook evenly from heat radiated by the sides as well as the bottom of the pot. ☐ The large, wide enameled cast-iron pot with slightly curved sides made by Le

fresh catch bouillabaisse

Creuset (see Purveyors, page 140) is best for this dish. Variously called a bouillabaisse pot, marmite, and **Dutch oven,** it conducts heat very well, which makes it an all-purpose pot. You will also need a medium **soup pot** to make the broth for this recipe.

serves 4 to 6

CROUTONS

Sixteen 1-inch-thick baguette slices

6 tablespoons extra-virgin olive oil, divided

5 garlic cloves, 2 whole and 3 minced

9 cups water

2 teaspoons salt

2 bay leaves

10 black peppercorns

1 large onion, minced

2 medium carrots, diced

2 leeks (white part only), washed thoroughly and minced

2 medium rutabagas, peeled and diced

1/2 medium fennel bulb (white part only), minced

1 medium parsnip, diced

2 medium celery ribs, diced

2 cups dry white wine

To make the croutons: Preheat the oven to 250°F. Arrange the bread in a single layer on a baking sheet. Brush or spray both sides of the bread with 2 tablespoons of the olive oil and then rub with the 2 whole cloves of garlic. Bake for 30 minutes, until the croutons are toasty brown. Remove the croutons from the oven and set aside.

Combine the water, salt, bay leaves, and peppercorns in a medium soup pot. Heat to a boil over medium heat, then reduce the heat and simmer, uncovered, for 30 minutes. Remove the broth from the heat and set aside.

Heat a large bouillabaisse pot over medium heat and add the remaining 4 tablespoons oil. Add the onion, carrots, and leeks. Sauté for 2 minutes. Add the rutabagas, fennel, parsnip, celery, and remaining 3 cloves minced garlic. Sauté for another 2 minutes, or until the vegetables begin to soften. Add the wine, tomatoes, potatoes, saffron, zest, rosemary, thyme, and pepper. Bring to a boil, stirring frequently. Strain the reserved broth through a strainer into the bouillabaisse pot. Bring to a boil again. Reduce the heat to low and carefully add the lobster, cod, snapper, and shrimp. Simmer for 10 minutes, covered, until the lobster tails are pink and the fish is opaque and cooked through. Remove the lid and carefully add the mussels, clams, and crab claws. Cover the pot and simmer for about 5 minutes, stirring occasionally, until the mussels and clams open and the claws are pink. (Discard any mussels or clams that do not open.)

Arrange 2 croutons in each of 6 to 8 deep, heavy soup bowls. Carefully transfer some of the seafood into the bowls with a slotted spoon and then ladle some broth and vegetables into the bowls.

1 pound plum tomatoes, seeded and chopped

8 ounces boiling potatoes, peeled and diced

2 teaspoons saffron threads

1 teaspoon grated orange zest

¾ teaspoon dried rosemary

¾ teaspoon dried thyme

¼ teaspoon freshly ground pepper

1 pound small lobster tails

1 pound cod fillets, cut into 2-inch pieces

1 pound red snapper fillets, cut into 2-inch pieces

1 pound medium shrimp (31–35), peeled and deveined

2 dozen (12 ounces) mussels, scrubbed and debearded

1 dozen (1 pound) littleneck clams, scrubbed

8 to 10 (1½ pounds) stone crab claws

You may use either clams or mussels for this dish. Use small clams like Manila or littleneck; for mussels, I prefer green-lip mussels from New Zealand. Make sure to scrub them very well. And, as always, any shellfish that does not open during cooking must be discarded. ☐ You will need a large, clad stainless steel **sauté pan** with a lid and a **pasta pentola** for the linguine, or else a soup pot and a colander. Keep an eye on your sauté pan—you don't want to overcook the shellfish. Have everything ready, and when the pasta water starts to boil, make the shellfish in the time it takes to cook the pasta.

lovers' linguine and shells

1½ teaspoons kosher salt

1 pound linguine

¼ cup olive oil

5 to 6 garlic cloves, chopped

¾ cup dry white wine

3 pounds clams or mussels, scrubbed (and if mussels, debearded)

½ cup chopped fresh flat-leaf parsley, divided

¼ cup fresh lemon juice

serves 4

Fill a pasta pentola three quarters full of water and bring to a boil over medium-high heat. Add the salt to the water and then the pasta. Cook according to the package instructions or to your taste.

Meanwhile, heat a large sauté pan over medium heat. Add the oil and then the garlic. Sauté for 1 minute, being careful not to cook the garlic too much. Add the wine and shellfish and toss well. Add half of the parsley and the lemon juice and toss again. Cover the sauté pan and steam the shellfish for 5 minutes, or until all the shells have opened. Uncover, discard any unopened shells, and reduce the heat to low.

Raise the insert of the pasta pentola and tilt it so the water drains into the pot. Rinse the pasta with fresh water, drain, and pour the pasta into the sauté pan with the shellfish.

Using tongs, toss the pasta with the shellfish and broth. Sprinkle the remaining parsley on top and serve immediately.

tantalizing turkey cutlets with
chanterelle cream sauce and brussels sprouts

2 tablespoons unbleached
    all-purpose flour

1 teaspoon kosher salt

¼ teaspoon freshly ground pepper

Eight 4-ounce turkey cutlets,
    pounded about ¼ inch thick

3 tablespoons clarified butter
    (ghee)

1 tablespoon minced shallot

2 garlic cloves, minced

2 cups (12 ounces) fresh
    chanterelle mushrooms,
    stemmed

BUTTERED BRUSSELS SPROUTS

3 cups (1½ pounds) Brussels
    sprouts

1 tablespoon clarified butter
    (ghee)

1 teaspoon caraway seeds

1½ teaspoons fresh lemon juice

½ cup dry white wine

1 cup heavy whipping cream

1 tablespoon chopped fresh
    flat-leaf parsley

Fresh lemon juice for drizzling

Chanterelle mushrooms are very sweet and add a fantastic flavor to the sauce in this turkey dish. Clarified butter, or ghee, is best for browning the turkey because it has a high smoke point; ghee can be found in most gourmet markets and all Indian markets. ☐ I use a large clad stainless steel **sauté pan** so I can scrape up the browned bits after cooking the turkey without harming the pan, and because the pan will not react with the acidic wine. ☐ As an accompaniment to the turkey, Brussels sprouts do not need much embellishment. If you want to serve them with something a bit less saucy, you can enhance their flavor with pancetta, Parmesan cheese, or nutmeg. A medium **saucepan** with a lid is perfect for this dish.

serves 4

Put the flour, salt, and pepper in a shallow bowl. Dredge the turkey cutlets in the mixture and shake off the excess. Heat 2 tablespoons of the butter in a large sauté pan over medium heat until hot but not smoking. Cook the cutlets on one side for 4 to 5 minutes, until golden. Turn and cook for 3 minutes more, until browned. Transfer the cutlets to a platter. Add another tablespoon of butter to the pan. Add the shallot, sauté for 3 minutes, and then add the garlic and sauté for 1 minute more, scraping up any bits from the bottom of the pan. Add the mushrooms and stir to coat well. Sauté the mushrooms for 3 to 4 minutes, until they begin to soften.

Meanwhile to prepare the Brussels sprouts: Trim the outer leaves and score them with an "X" on the bottom of each stem. Put them in a medium saucepan barely covered with water. Heat over medium heat to a light simmer—do not boil rapidly. Cook for only 4 to 5 minutes, just until fork-tender. Drain and immediately add the butter and caraway seeds. Cover, toss well to coat, and set aside. Just before serving, drizzle the lemon juice over the top.

At the same time, add the wine to the mushroom pan and allow it to reduce by half, about 5 minutes. Add the cream and allow it to reduce by half, about 5 minutes more. Return the cutlets to the pan, spooning the sauce on top to coat very well. Drizzle with lemon juice and top with the parsley. Serve immediately with the Buttered Brussels Sprouts.

If desserts tend to be sort of ho-hum at your house, this chapter will get you out of your rut. Instead of baking cupcakes for a children's party, how about *Sweetart Suckers*, which will make good use of your saucier pan? In the time it takes to run out and buy a pie for dinner, you can

create elegant *Poached Pears Drizzled with Beaujolais Sauce* with the help of the trusty sauté pan. If you're looking for a showstopper, I'll teach you how to flambé brandy for the spectacular *Flaming Cherries Jubilee*. Some of the treats in this chapter will also make delicious gifts. Your friends will love to receive a box of *Tipsy Toffee*, which requires just a saucepan and a baking sheet. I even included some opportunities to get the kids involved—that is always fun!

Be careful when you add the baking soda at the end of the cooking time for this addictive hard candy, as it causes vigorous bubbling! Store the candy in jars or airtight tins at room temperature; exposure to moisture and air will soften it. Once you become comfortable with this basic recipe, try flavoring it with a few drops of your favorite fruit essence, available at most supermarkets in the baking section. ☐ A large clad stainless steel **saucepan** is the only pan for this recipe, as it will not react to the vinegar. You will also need a 9-inch square cake pan and a candy thermometer, which clips on easily to the straight side of the saucepan. No yield is given in this recipe because it varies, depending on how you break it.

i want candy candy

SPECIAL EQUIPMENT
clip-on candy thermometer

Unsalted butter for greasing foil

1 cup sugar

1 cup dark corn syrup

1 tablespoon distilled white vinegar

½ tablespoon fruit flavoring

1 tablespoon baking soda, sifted

makes 1 pound

Line a 9-by-9-by-2-inch square cake pan with foil, extending it over the sides. Butter the foil generously. Combine the sugar, corn syrup, and vinegar in a large, heavy, deep saucepan and clip a candy thermometer to the side. Heat over medium heat, stirring constantly, until the sugar dissolves. Continue simmering, without stirring, but swirling the mixture in the pan occasionally, until the candy thermometer registers 300°F, about 15 minutes. Stir in the flavoring and remove the pan from the heat. Immediately add the baking soda and stir until well combined (it will foam vigorously). Quickly pour the mixture into the prepared pan. Cool completely at room temperature until the candy is hard.

To unmold the candy: Using the foil as an aid, lift the candy from the pan and fold down the foil sides. Cut or break the candy into large pieces, peeling the foil off. Store in an airtight container for up to one week.

Everyone loves this dessert named for Richard Foster, a 1950s regular at the famous New Orleans restaurant Brennan's. Try some of the special varieties of bananas on the market today, especially the little red ones, which are sweeter than common yellow ones. I prefer using Captain Morgan's Spiced Rum with its sweet-spicy kick. Serve this with vanilla ice cream sprinkled with a little grated sweetened coconut on top if you like. ☐ A large nonstick **fry pan** is the best choice for this dessert so the caramel will not stick. A heat-resistant spatula will be a helpful aid in scraping up all the sauce to pour over the ice cream.

ooh baby bananas foster

4 tablespoons unsalted butter

½ cup packed dark brown sugar

2 tablespoons dark rum

2 bananas, peeled and sliced
in half lengthwise

1 quart vanilla ice cream

serves 4

Melt the butter in a large nonstick fry pan over medium heat. Add the brown sugar and rum. Stir well to dissolve the sugar and bring to a boil. Once the butter-rum mixture begins to thicken, in about 3 minutes, add the bananas and gently spoon the mixture over the bananas to coat them very well. Cook for 1 minute to warm them, and remove the pan from the heat. Cool the bananas and syrup for about 2 minutes while you dish up the ice cream. Spoon over the ice cream and serve immediately.

No store-bought brand compares with homemade hot fudge sauce. Make an ice cream sundae bar for your next party with the best-quality vanilla ice cream you can find and lots of topping goodies. You can increase the quantity of sauce to infinity. Melting chocolate in a **double boiler** is a breeze. Keep the water in the bottom of the double boiler at a mild simmer so it does not disturb the top pot. No water should bubble into the chocolate, though, or the hot fudge could stiffen up!

hot hot fudge sundaes

One 5-ounce can evaporated milk (about ⅔ cup)

¾ cup sugar

2 ounces unsweetened chocolate, chopped

2 tablespoons unsalted butter

2 tablespoons light corn syrup

1½ teaspoons vanilla

⅛ teaspoon kosher salt

1 quart vanilla ice cream

Whipped cream for garnish

Ice cream sprinkles for garnish

Chopped nuts for garnish

serves 4; makes about 1 cup sauce

Fill the bottom of a double boiler halfway (about 3 inches) with water and heat to a low simmer. Heat the evaporated milk and sugar in the top of the double boiler, stirring, until the sugar is dissolved.

Add the chocolate, butter, and corn syrup to the milk mixture and continue to cook, stirring constantly, just until the chocolate is melted. Bring the mixture to a boil, stirring occasionally, and then simmer for 10 minutes.

Remove the pan from the heat and stir in the vanilla and salt. Cool the sauce completely before covering and refrigerating. The fudge sauce will keep, covered, in the refrigerator for 3 weeks. Reheat the sauce, uncovered, over simmering water in a double boiler.

To serve, dish the ice cream into chilled bowls. Drizzle the Hot Hot Fudge Sauce on top and garnish with whipped cream, sprinkles, and nuts.

In almost every fine dining restaurant in the sixties, this dessert was served tableside in a chafing dish, flames rising to the ceiling and patrons gasping and wanting the same drama at their table. So, let's flambé! Although it sounds so dramatic, it is really pretty simple. Just practice and be careful. For safety, I like to use a butane igniter with a long stem, available at almost every supermarket and hardware store. Vanilla beans and quality frozen cherries are easily available—look for the best in gourmet markets. For cherries, I prefer Ocean Spray (see Purveyors, page 140). ☐ Use a small, nonreactive stainless steel **saucepan** to heat the kirsch and a large clad stainless steel **fry pan** to flambé. Never use a nonstick pan for flambéing; it will damage the interior. Practice igniting the kirsch a couple of times, if you like, to get comfortable with the flame. And, if you have long hair, by all means pull it back.

flaming cherries jubilee

SPECIAL EQUIPMENT
fire starter, long-handled stainless steel spoon, and long-handled stainless steel ladle

serves 4

½ cup kirsch

One 16-ounce package frozen pitted Bing cherries, thawed in a strainer over a bowl

2 cups plus 2 tablespoons natural unsweetened cherry juice, divided (see Purveyors, page 140)

½ cup dried cranberries

2 tablespoons superfine sugar

1 vanilla bean

1 tablespoon arrowroot

1 tablespoon minced orange zest

1 quart vanilla ice cream

Heat the kirsch over very low heat in a small saucepan. Pour the juice that collected in the bowl below the thawing cherries into a large fry pan. Add 2 cups of the cherry juice, the cranberries, and sugar to the pan and bring to a simmer over medium heat. As the mixture begins to bubble, use the tip of a paring knife to split the vanilla bean length-wise and scrape the tiny vanilla seeds into the pan. Continue to simmer, stirring occasionally, until the mixture is reduced by half, about 15 minutes. Mix the arrowroot with the remaining 2 tablespoons cherry juice and stir into the pan. Simmer the mixture until thickened, about 1 minute. Stir in the cherries and the zest. Remove the pan from the heat. Scoop the ice cream into dessert dishes.

continued

Carefully pour the kirsch into a large ladle. Ignite the kirsch and pour it into the cherry mixture. Immediately stir well with a long-handled stainless steel spoon until the flames go out. Quickly spoon the mixture over the ice cream and serve.

variation

Spoon the finished cherry mixture into Authentic Crêpes (page 26), fold each crêpe over, and sprinkle with powdered sugar.

These little treats will give you a bit of a jolt because of the espresso, so don't eat too many—share! ☐ A **double boiler** is best for melting the chocolate. As always, watch the temperature of the water; you want just a slow simmer so the water does not seep into the top pan with the chocolate. Wipe the inside of the top pan very well with butter beforehand for easy cleanup. You will also need a small baking pan.

grand marnier–laced chocolate truffles

makes about 50 truffles

SPECIAL EQUIPMENT
1-ounce scoop

- 1 tablespoon instant espresso powder
- 1 tablespoon boiling water
- 12 ounces good-quality bittersweet chocolate (not unsweetened), chopped
- 4 tablespoons unsalted butter, cut into pieces, plus extra for coating the pan
- ¼ cup heavy whipping cream
- 2 tablespoons Grand Marnier or other orange liqueur
- 1 cup unsweetened cocoa powder for coating truffles

Butter a small 9-inch baking pan and dissolve the espresso in the water. Fill the bottom of a double boiler halfway (about 3 inches) with water and heat over medium-low heat until just simmering. Add the chocolate and butter to the top of the double boiler. Once they begin to melt, add the cream and espresso, stirring until smooth. Remove the top of the double boiler from the heat and stir in the Grand Marnier. Pour the mixture into the buttered baking pan. Cool the truffle mixture at room temperature for about 20 minutes and then refrigerate, covered, at least 3 hours, or until firm.

Select an airtight container to hold the finished truffles. Cut sheets of wax paper to fit inside the container.

Using a 1-ounce scoop, form the chocolate mixture into balls and roll the balls in the cocoa powder, coating them. Line the airtight container with a layer of wax paper. Make a single layer of finished truffles, being careful not to crowd them. Place a sheet of wax paper on top and continue making layers in this way. The truffles will keep, refrigerated, for up to 2 weeks.

The coating for the apples is a classic caramel that must be cooked with patience. Once you make these, try additional toppings on top of the caramel, such as chocolate bits and nuts. This is a great opportunity to develop a signature flavor combination. Make sure that the apples are firm and crisp. These are best made and eaten within a day, but they will keep, refrigerated, for up to one week. ☐ A large clad stainless steel or anodized aluminum **saucier pan** is most convenient so you will have plenty of room to dip the apples and the whisk can easily slide around the curved sides. The trick is to keep your flame low and watch the temperature of the caramel.

sticky sweet caramel apples

SPECIAL EQUIPMENT
clip-on candy thermometer, pastry brush, 12 wooden chopsticks

1 cup (2 sticks) unsalted butter, at room temperature, plus extra for greasing foil

One 1-pound box dark brown sugar

One 14-ounce can sweetened condensed milk

⅔ cup dark corn syrup

⅓ cup pure maple syrup

1½ teaspoons vanilla extract

1 teaspoon dark molasses

¼ teaspoon kosher salt

12 medium Granny Smith or other crisp apples

Chopped nuts, candy bar pieces, sprinkles, and other toppings (optional)

serves 6

Heat the butter in a large saucier or saucepan over medium heat. Add the sugar, milk, corn syrup, maple syrup, vanilla, molasses, and salt. Cook the mixture for about 15 minutes, stirring with a wooden spoon, until the sugar dissolves. Brush down the insides of the pan with a moist pastry brush to prevent sugar crystals from forming. Test the caramel by rubbing a little between your fingers. If it is smooth and free of "grit" from the sugar, it is ready for the next stage. Attach the candy thermometer to the side of the pan and heat the caramel to 235°F, stirring occasionally with a wooden spoon and brushing down the sides of the pan with the moist pastry brush. This should take about 15 minutes. Pour the caramel into a glass or nonreactive metal bowl and transfer the thermometer to the bowl. Allow the caramel to cool, without stirring, until the thermometer reads 200°F. This should take 15 to 20 minutes.

While the caramel cools, line a baking sheet with foil and butter the foil very well. Push a chopstick into the stem end of each apple. Holding the chopstick, dip an apple into the caramel up to the chopstick, and allow the caramel to drip off. Place the apple on the buttered foil and repeat with the remaining apples. Allow the apples to set for about 15 minutes, and then lift the apples off the foil one at a time, turning the apple slowly to collect any pooled caramel on the foil. If you like, dip the apples into or drizzle with melted chocolate, and roll them in nuts or other goodies. Allow the apples to set for another hour before serving.

Indulgence in a cup! Take note of the chilling time—make this in the morning to serve with dinner, and it will have plenty of time to set. ☐ A medium **saucier pan,** which allows you to whisk easily, and a couple of mixing bowls—perhaps copper for the egg whites—are all you need for this decadent dessert. A heat-resistant spatula is also a useful tool for gently folding egg whites into the chocolate mousse mixture and for scraping up every bit of sweet mousse. You will be making this often once you discover how simple it is.

chocolate mousse

1½ cups heavy whipping cream

½ cup whole milk

¼ cup sugar

3 large eggs, separated

1 tablespoon unbleached
all-purpose flour

4 tablespoons unsalted butter

One 6-ounce package semisweet
chocolate chips

1 tablespoon pure vanilla extract

1½ tablespoons grated orange zest

serves 6 to 8 generously

In a medium bowl, beat the cream until very stiff peaks form. In a medium saucier or saucepan, whisk together the milk, sugar, egg yolks, and flour. Heat over medium heat, whisking constantly, until the mixture is the consistency of custard, about 5 minutes. Add the butter one tablespoon at a time, stirring after each addition. Remove the pan from the heat, add the chocolate, and stir vigorously until the chocolate is melted and the mixture is well blended. Stir in the vanilla and orange zest. Allow the mixture to cool slightly.

In a medium copper or nonreactive metal bowl, beat the egg whites until stiff peaks form. Gently fold the egg whites into the chocolate mixture and then fold in half of the whipped cream until well distributed. (Do not beat.) Spoon the mousse into sherbet dishes and chill until firm, about 5 hours. Serve each with a dollop of the remaining whipped cream.

Homemade suckers are special, a chance to show off your style or celebrate a special occasion. The sucker molds, sticks, flavoring oil, and coloring can be ordered from several manufacturers found on the Internet (see Purveyors, page 140). You will also want to have some cellophane and ribbon on hand to wrap the suckers. ☐ A medium clad stainless steel **saucepan** or saucier works perfectly for making these treats. It is nonreactive, in case you will be using citrus flavorings, easy to clean, and heavy, so you can regulate the temperature for even cooking.

sweetart suckers

makes about twelve 3-inch suckers

SPECIAL EQUIPMENT
clip-on candy thermometer, sucker molds, sucker sticks

Spray the molds with nonstick spray. Combine the sugar, water, and corn syrup in a medium saucepan and bring to a boil over medium heat. Attach the candy thermometer to the pan, and boil until the thermometer reads 290°F. Remove the saucepan from the heat. When the bubbles simmer down, stir in the flavoring and coloring as desired. Carefully pour the hot candy mixture into the prepared molds. Remove the suckers from the molds when they are cool and beginning to hold their shape, after about 15 minutes. Add some decorations if desired. Place the suckers on a flat surface covered with wax paper to continue cooling. Wrap the cooled suckers in cellophane, tie each one with a ribbon, and store the suckers in sealed plastic bags for up to 2 weeks.

Good-quality nonstick cooking spray for greasing

1 cup sugar

½ cup water

⅓ cup light corn syrup

⅛ to ¼ teaspoon candy flavoring oil

Liquid food coloring, as desired

Candy eyes and/or decorations (optional; see Purveyors, page 140)

It is so wonderful to give and receive food gifts. This is one of my favorites to wrap up during the holidays and on other special occasions. ☐ You will need a large, heavy **saucepan** for this recipe, and a medium baking sheet with a lip. Watch your heat under the saucepan. If your stove has a powerful gas flame, you may want to use a diffuser—a metal disk that sits on top of the flame to temper the direct heat.

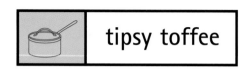

tipsy toffee

makes about 2 pounds of toffee

SPECIAL EQUIPMENT
clip-on candy thermometer

1¼ cups (2½ sticks) unsalted butter

1 cup sugar

½ cup packed light brown sugar

⅓ cup water

1 tablespoon light molasses

½ teaspoon kosher salt

¼ teaspoon ground allspice

2 cups (1 pound) slivered
   almonds, divided

5 ounces good-quality bittersweet
   chocolate, coarsely chopped

Line a large baking sheet with foil and use some of the butter to coat it generously. Melt the remaining butter in a large saucepan over low heat. Add the sugars, water, molasses, salt, and allspice and stir constantly with a wooden spoon until the sugars dissolve. Attach the candy thermometer to the pan. Increase the heat to medium and boil the mixture until the thermometer registers 290°F, stirring slowly but constantly and scraping the bottom of the pan with the spoon, about 20 minutes. Remove the pan from the heat. Mix in 1½ cups of the almonds. Immediately pour the candy onto the foil-lined baking sheet. Using the wooden spoon, spread out the toffee to an even ¼ inch. Quickly sprinkle the chocolate pieces over the toffee and allow the chocolate to melt from the heat of the toffee, about 1 minute. Using the back of the wooden spoon, spread out the chocolate over the toffee. Sprinkle with the remaining ½ cup almonds. Refrigerate, uncovered, for 1 hour. With the help of the foil, lift the toffee out of the baking sheet and break it into pieces. Divide among cellophane bags and secure each one with a ribbon. The toffee can be made 2 weeks ahead. Once it is broken into pieces, the toffee can be stored in an airtight container for 2 weeks. Let stand at room temperature at least 30 minutes and up to 1 hour before serving.

Zabaglione, like sabayon, is a whipped sweetened egg mixture. I like to serve this dessert after a heavy meal because it is so light and very easy to make. The custard base is delicate and should be made in a **double boiler,** particularly copper, if you have it. Watch the temperature of the water, which must be kept at a steady simmer. Have a large bowl handy so that you can quickly add some ice and water when they are needed.

silky zabaglione and berries

serves 4 to 6

Fill the bottom of a double boiler halfway (about 3 inches) with water and heat to a mellow simmer over medium heat, but do not add the top pan yet. Using a whisk or an electric hand mixer, beat the egg yolks, sugar, and salt in the top of the double boiler. Now set the top over the bottom of the double boiler, clip on the thermometer, and gradually beat in the wine. Continue beating until the mixture holds its shape on a spoon and the candy thermometer reads 160°F, about 10 minutes. Set the top of the double boiler into a large bowl filled with ice water. Whisk the egg mixture until it is cool. Remove the pan from the ice water and set aside. In a medium glass or nonreactive metal bowl, beat the cream with the whisk or electric hand mixer until stiff peaks form. Add the crème de cassis and beat until stiff peaks form again. Fold the whipped cream into the egg mixture. Cover and refrigerate for at least 1 hour, until firm, and for no more than 4 hours.

To serve, divide the berries among 4 to 6 plates, spoon the zabaglione on top, and serve immediately.

SPECIAL EQUIPMENT
clip-on candy thermometer

 3 large egg yolks

 ¼ cup sugar

 ¼ teaspoon kosher salt

 ½ cup dry white wine

 ½ cup heavy whipping cream

 5 tablespoons crème de cassis
 liqueur

 1 pint (8 ounces) fresh
 raspberries

 1 pint (8 ounces) fresh
 blueberries

This is a stylish and easy dessert to make ahead of time. Peaches can be used instead of pears if they are in season. The fruit should be perfectly ripe—not too soft, not too hard. Baste the pears often so they soak up the sauce. ☐ I use a large clad stainless steel or anodized aluminum **sauté pan** for this dessert so I have plenty of room for basting and the pan will not react with the wine.

poached pears drizzled with beaujolais sauce

1 ½ cups Beaujolais wine

½ cup sugar

1 cinnamon stick

3 whole cloves

Two 3-inch strips lemon zest, plus grated zest for garnish

4 ripe pears

Fresh mint sprigs for garnish

serves 4

Combine the wine, sugar, cinnamon stick, cloves, and zest strips in a large sauté pan. Bring the mixture to a boil over medium heat and cook, stirring occasionally, for about 5 minutes. The sugar should be dissolved and the sauce will have begun to thicken. While the sauce is cooking, peel, halve, and core the pears. Add the pears to the sauce and spoon it over the pears to generously coat them. Cover, remove the pan from the heat, and set the pan on a trivet. Allow the mixture to cool to room temperature, about 30 minutes. Transfer the fruit and syrup to an airtight container and refrigerate until well chilled, at least 2 hours and no more than 3 days. To serve, remove the cinnamon stick, cloves, and lemon zest and divide the fruit and sauce among 4 bowls. Garnish each serving with grated lemon zest and a mint sprig.

aidells gourmet sausages
1625 Alvarado Street
San Leandro, CA 94577
www.aidells.com
Purveyors of gourmet sausages

purveyors

all-clad metalcrafters
424 Morganza Road
Canonsburg, PA 15317
(800) 255-2523
www.allclad.com
Makers of clad stainless steel, clad stainless steel nonstick, and copper cookware

confectionary house
www.confectionaryhouse.com
Quality supplies for the serious baker, cake decorator, and candy maker

kitchenaid
P.O. Box 2128
St. Joseph, MI 49085
(800) 541-6300
www.kitchenaid.com
Manufacturers of fine housewares

le creuset of america
1 Bob Gifford Boulevard
Early Branch, SC 29916
(803) 943-4308
www.lecreuset.com
Manufacturers of the finest enameled cast-iron cookware and bakeware

lodge manufacturing company
P.O. Box 380
South Pittsburg, TN 37380
(615) 837-7181
www.lodge.com
Manufacturers of cast-iron bakeware and cookware

melissa's / world variety produce, inc.
P.O. Box 21127
Los Angeles, CA 90021
(800) 588-0151
www.melissas.com
Suppliers of fine produce

oceanspray cranberries, inc.
One Oceanspray Drive
Lakeville-Middleboro, MA 02349
www.oceanspray.com
Purveyors of cranberry and other fruit products

rösle
841 East Fillmore
East Aurora, NY 14052
(716) 655-4131
Manufacturers of fine kitchen tools

servaas laboratories
1200 Waterway Boulevard
Indianapolis, IN 46202
(800) 433-5818
www.barkeepersfriend.com
Manufacturers of cleaning products including Bar Keepers Friend

The exact equivalents in the following tables have been rounded for convenience.

table of equivalents

LIQUID/DRY MEASURES

U.S.	Metric
¼ teaspoon	1.25 milliliters
½ teaspoon	2.5 milliliters
1 teaspoon	5 milliliters
1 tablespoon (3 teaspoons)	15 milliliters
1 fluid ounce (2 tablespoons)	30 milliliters
¼ cup	60 milliliters
⅓ cup	80 milliliters
½ cup	120 milliliters
1 cup	240 milliliters
1 pint (2 cups)	480 milliliters
1 quart (4 cups, 32 ounces)	960 milliliters
1 gallon (4 quarts)	3.84 liters
1 ounce (by weight)	28 grams
1 pound	454 grams
2.2 pounds	1 kilogram

LENGTH

U.S.	Metric
⅛ inch	3 millimeters
¼ inch	6 millimeters
½ inch	12 millimeters
1 inch	2.5 centimeters

OVEN TEMPERATURE

Fahrenheit	Celsius	Gas
250	120	½
275	140	1
300	150	2
325	160	3
350	180	4
375	190	5
400	200	6
425	220	7
450	230	8
475	240	9
500	260	10